THE GOSPEL OF MARK
NOW STREAMING AT

WWW.RIGHTNOWMEDIA.ORG/MARK

© 2018 by RightNow Ministries International

Published by RightNow Ministries International
6300 Henneman Way
McKinney, TX 75070
www.rightnow.org

ISBN - 978-0-692-19327-3

Scripture quotations are from the ESV® Bible (The
Holy Bible, English Standard Version®), copyright ©
2001 by Crossway, a publishing ministry of Good News
Publishers. Used by permission. All rights reserved.

Cover photo © Elijah Hiett, used with permission. All
other photography © RightNow Ministries.

THE GOSPEL OF

MARK

It's hard to call it "work" when your job means traveling to Israel with Francis Chan. Traveling all over the Holy Land, our team had an unforgettable experience filming Francis teaching through the Gospel of Mark.

This picture is one of my favorites from the entire trip. It's not a scenic skyline of Jerusalem or an epic shot of the Sea of Galilee. It's our team huddled together after the last camera stopped rolling. Standing on that rooftop with my hand on Francis's shoulder, I prayed that God would use this whole resource to help people get into Scripture and to deepen their relationship with God.

Our team has worked hard to create the videos and study guide that will help you journey through the book of Mark. The videos will give you a glimpse into the places where Jesus walked. The study guide will help you dive in to Mark's gospel and experience Scripture for yourself.

I hope you don't rush. Pace yourself and ask God how he wants you to respond to this book of the Bible that chronicles the life and ministry of Jesus.

The mission of the church matters!

Brian Mosley
President, RightNow Ministries

HOW TO USE THIS STUDY GUIDE

Welcome to the study guide for RightNow Media's *The Gospel of Mark*, featuring Francis Chan. What you hold in your hands is meant to be more than an intellectual analysis of Mark's gospel. It's a journey intended to lead you along in the footsteps of Jesus as he walks the road from Galilee to Jerusalem. This guide will require more of you than simply reading the Bible and answering a few questions. It'll ask you to engage your heart and your hands as well—feeling the full impact of Mark's writing as well as putting into action the challenges his gospel makes to his reader.

This guide is broken out into eleven weeks, each one corresponding to the video Bible study series. There are five days' worth of devotional activities per week that will both dig into the text of the gospel as well as offer opportunities to put into practice the life-changing truths in Mark's words. It's up to you how you break up the days across your week. The first day of each week focuses specifically on Francis's teaching, with questions to encourage engagement with the video and discussion if you're using the study in a group setting.

Each week begins with three goals: life change in your mind, your emotions, and your actions. Everything that follows in the week aims at helping you practically apply the truths in Mark's gospel to your life.

Throughout the guide, you'll find bolded questions or action points that ask you to do something with what you're studying. There's also space in the guide to write down notes, prayers, or answers to questions.

You'll find a small number corresponding to the question in that space, which should help you keep track of what item your writing refers to. You're definitely not limited to that space, however. This book is just a guide.

As you work through the book, you'll find more than just the words on the page. Francis's teaching in each video session will set up the week for you and help orient you to that week's passage. You'll also encounter deeper looks at the original language in Mark's gospel, as well as maps and other helpful explanations of sticky issues.

If you're using this book as part of a group study, consider watching the video teaching together and discussing the questions found in the first day during your group time. Then, throughout the week, work through the remaining four days of questions. When you get together again, talk through your week's study before moving on to the next session.

In the end, this book is a guide on a journey. Mark's gospel works like a travel journal, following Jesus as he leads his stumbling disciples along the path of discipleship. The guide you hold in your hands, along with the teaching from Francis Chan, will lead you along that same path. At the end of the journey—and at the end of this book—you'll have a very important question to answer: Will you follow Jesus?

WEEKLY GOALS
Each week begins with three life change goals aimed at your mind, emotions, and actions.

VIDEO SESSSIONS
Begin each week by watching the corresponding video session.

ACTION POINTS
Each day's questions and challenges are marked with small numbers to help you stay organized.

JOURNAL SECTION
There's space in the guide to write down notes, prayers, or answers to questions.

TABLE OF CONTENTS

THE RIVER JORDAN

The Jordan River symbolized new beginnings for the people of Israel. John the Baptist's ministry in the river called the nation to repentance—a new start. At his own baptism, Jesus announced the beginning of his own ministry. God the Father and the Spirit confirmed Jesus's identity as he rose from the water. The Messiah had come.

SESSION 1:

Mark 1:1–13

Welcome to Mark's gospel. When we open the pages of this powerful presentation of Jesus, we're stepping out onto a road. We're taking a journey from the shore of the Sea of Galilee to the streets of Jerusalem running red with Jesus's blood.

In this study, we're going to follow Jesus. Along the way, we'll discover more about the God-Man who came to die, yes. But we'll also discover more about ourselves and the barriers we put up along the road of discipleship.

When we study the Bible, our ultimate goal is to walk away changed. We want to know more about our God and what we can do to become and act more like his Son, Jesus.

In this first week, we'll dig into one main idea: Jesus Christ is unlike any other savior. He is the champion—the savior—all of humanity has longed for.

That idea has the potential to change how we think, feel, and behave.

- We want to understand that Jesus Christ is holy, unlike any other.
- We want to feel fascinated with the good news of Jesus Christ.
- We want to actively make Jesus Christ the priority of our lives.

As we go through this week's study in Mark, keep those objectives in mind.

WATCH: THE GOSPEL OF MARK WITH FRANCIS CHAN, SESSION 1

DAY ONE

As you begin this series, think about what you'd like to learn or ways in which you'd like to grow. [1] **Take a moment to write down two things you'd like to take away from the book of Mark in the space below.**

1

¹The beginning of the gospel of Jesus Christ, the Son of God. ²As it is written in Isaiah the prophet,

"Behold, I send my messenger before your face,
*   who will prepare your way,*
³the voice of one crying in the wilderness:
*   'Prepare the way of the Lord,*
*   make his paths straight,'"*

⁴John appeared, baptizing in the wilderness and proclaiming a baptism of repentance for the forgiveness of sins.
⁵And all the country of Judea and all Jerusalem were going out to him and were being baptized by him in the river
Jordan, confessing their sins. ⁶Now John was clothed with camel's hair and wore a leather belt around his waist
and ate locusts and wild honey. ⁷And he preached, saying, "After me comes he who is mightier than I, the strap of
whose sandals I am not worthy to stoop down and untie. ⁸I have baptized you with water, but he will baptize you
with the Holy Spirit."

⁹In those days Jesus came from Nazareth of Galilee and was baptized by John in the Jordan. ¹⁰And when he
came up out of the water, immediately he saw the heavens being torn open and the Spirit descending on him like
a dove. ¹¹And a voice came from heaven, "You are my beloved Son; with you I am well pleased."

MARK 1:1–11

We don't study the Bible by ourselves. God has promised that his Spirit will open our eyes to the truths in his Word.

² Before we dive in, jot down a one-sentence prayer asking the Spirit to change you over the next few weeks as we journey through Mark.

Let's dive into the book. Open your Bible to the book of Mark and read 1:1–11.

Mark opens by setting the stage for Jesus. The word he uses is "gospel." Most of us have heard the term a thousand times. But here, Mark means he's about to tell the story of a victor. And in these first few verses, we get the origin story for this man who will save the world.

³ Reading these opening verses, what do you expect from Jesus? What kinds of things do you anticipate from him?

There's something special about Jesus—and John the Baptist gets it. Francis explained by pointing out how, in preparing for this series, he shared in the same angst as John in announcing the truth of Jesus.

Whether we feel it or not, the coming of Jesus to our world is a big deal.

[4] **So, who is Jesus to you? What kind of savior has he been? What do you want him to be?**

Over the next few weeks, we're going to encounter Jesus. We'll walk with him from Galilee to Jerusalem. The carpenter's shop to the cross. The question we'll have to answer at the end is whether or not we want to share in Jesus's story.

After all, it's good news. ∎

4

"

I sure hope this hasn't gotten old to you—the thought of God Almighty becoming flesh, emptying himself. The thought that I, right now, even have the right to speak about him. These are holy, holy, holy things.

"

DAY TWO

When it comes to studying any book of the Bible, it's good to start with some background. Today, we'll take a brief look at the historical context and purpose behind the Gospel of Mark.

AUTHOR

Of the Gospels, Mark is easily the shortest. It's also anonymous. The gospel itself does not specifically name "Mark" as its author, but the bulk of church history since the second century AD has affirmed it. Most likely, the same John Mark who traveled with Paul during his missionary journeys wrote this gospel.

For more information about John Mark, see: Acts 12:12, 25; 13:5, 13; 15:37–39; Col. 4:10; Phlm. 24; 2 Tim. 4:11; 1 Pet. 5:13.

PURPOSE

Writing from Rome in the first century, Mark penned his gospel following two major themes: 1) a thorough look at Jesus and 2) the true nature of discipleship. Mark wrote to a largely Gentile audience. He went out of his way to explain Jewish customs and describe Jesus as both the Jewish Messiah and the savior of the Gentiles. Even more, he emphasized the suffering and death of Jesus as the means by which we enter into a right relationship with God by faith. And the path of Jesus is the path we follow in true discipleship.

Mark wrote to Gentiles. John the Baptist spoke to Jews. Both wanted people to understand that Jesus was the most important person anyone could ever meet.

Let's do some journaling. Imagine you're Mark. You have this story about the amazing man Jesus burning a hole in your brain. You have to get it out.

[1] **Who would you write or tell the story to?**

[2] **What would you say about Jesus to get their attention?**

Think about this: The gospel you are studying was written close to 2,000 years ago because Mark was captivated by Jesus Christ. Inspired by the Holy Spirit, he wrote these words so that others would be able to encounter the savior in the same way. Ask God to give you a chance over the next few weeks to share this story of Jesus the God-Man with someone. ∎

1

2

Mediterranean
Sea

GALILEE

CAPERNAUM ★ ★ BETHSAIDA

★ CANA

Sea of
Galilee

★ NAZARETH

DECAPOLIS

★ CAESAREA

THE JORDAN RIVER

★ *The Jordan River is a relatively small river, rarely spanning more than fifteen yards across at any given point. Its main section runs the sixty-six miles from the Sea of Galilee to the Dead Sea. Aside from an occasional seasonal flood, the river isn't very deep.*

SAMARIA

★ JOPPA   ★ ARIMATHEA

PHILADELPHIA ★

JUDEA

JERICHO ★

PEREA

EMMAUS ★

JERUSALEM ★   ★ BETHANY

BETHLEHEM ★

Dead
Sea

★ HEBRON

IDUMEA

0 mi   20

0 km   20

DAY THREE

Today we're going to spend some time digging into the text of the passage we've been looking at. One of the most important tools for studying the Bible is a careful eye—observing the text.

We're looking for things in the words and sentences and paragraphs that are important to the author. So let's go back to Mark 1:1–13.

A long-foretold savior needs qualifications—and Mark clearly believes Jesus has those qualifications in spades. [1] **Read through the passage slowly and identify 3–4 things that Mark believes qualifies Jesus to be the savior of his people.**

We've already hinted at the interpretation of these first verses: Jesus is a big deal. He's *the* big deal. He's a big deal because prophets expected him, God confirmed him, and Jesus came through temptation a champion, not a failure.

But so what? What does this have to do with how you and I live our lives? We can answer that question by answering a different one:

[2] **Does Mark convince you? Is Jesus the Son of God, the savior? What evidence would Mark need to include in the rest of his book for you to be convinced?**

As you go through your day, think about the things you take as self-evident: A chair will hold you. A door that says "pull" opens toward you. Whether we've known Jesus all our lives or are only just now meeting him, we have the opportunity to decide for ourselves if we'll follow him.

Because if he's going to be the one leading us on the road of discipleship, he had better be qualified. ∎

2

> "We're talking about something so sacred in the book of Mark. The Creator of the universe loved us so much that he emptied himself of all of his glory. And he came down to this earth to pursue us."

DAY FOUR

Israel is a beautiful country, both for its landscape and its memorable history. Jesus walked across its soil in human flesh, and the faith we claim today sprang forth as a result. And it's staggering to consider that truth in comparison to how widespread Christianity is today.

Take a moment to reflect on your journey of faith up to this point. [1] **What are the major milestones in your life that led you to your current standing with Jesus?**

1

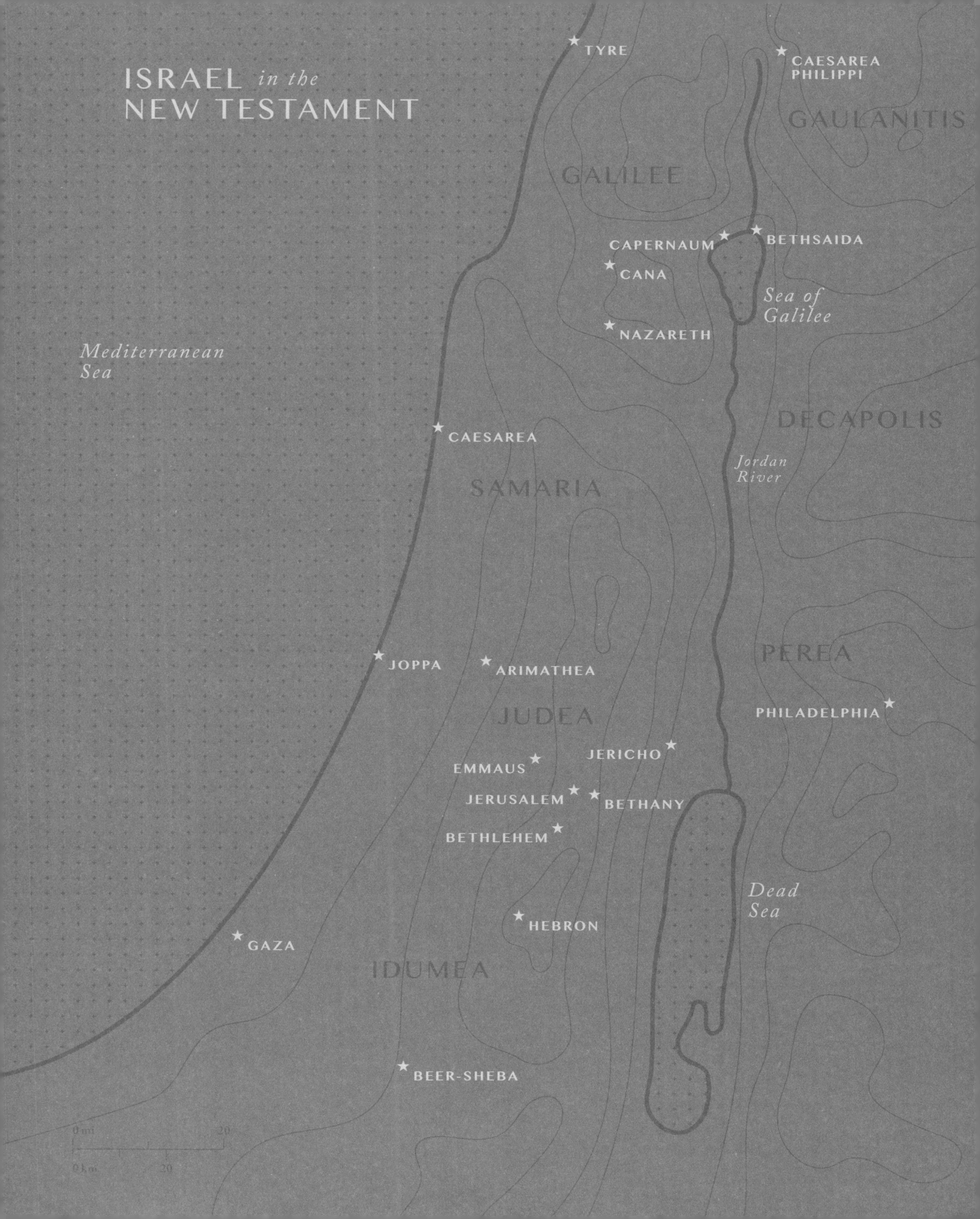

ISRAEL *in the* NEW TESTAMENT

Mediterranean Sea

TYRE

★ CAESAREA PHILIPPI

GAULANITIS

GALILEE

CAPERNAUM ★ ★ BETHSAIDA

★ CANA

Sea of Galilee

★ NAZARETH

DECAPOLIS

★ CAESAREA

SAMARIA

Jordan River

PEREA

★ JOPPA

★ ARIMATHEA

JUDEA

PHILADELPHIA ★

★ JERICHO

EMMAUS ★

JERUSALEM ★ ★ BETHANY

BETHLEHEM ★

★ HEBRON

Dead Sea

★ GAZA

IDUMEA

★ BEER-SHEBA

0 mi   20

0 km.   20

Now, think about the circumstances God has orchestrated to reveal himself to you. He placed specific people in your life to teach you about the faith. He did the same for those people and the people before them as well. All of it started with the story you're studying in Mark and the place introduced in these images. You have the opportunity to know Jesus Christ today because his disciples were captivated by him, so much so that they shared his truth with others. And that truth crossed borders, transcended languages, and travelled across oceans to reach you, all because of people who believed in the need to tell others about this Jesus.

PEEK AT THE GREEK ευαγγελιον

Despite being the shortest of the Gospels, Mark uses the term *euangelion* ("gospel") more than all of the others combined. It appears seven times (1:1, 14, 15, 8:35, 10:29, 13:10, 14:9) compared to Matthew's four. Neither Luke nor John uses the word in their accounts. Clearly, Mark intends to emphasize the "gospel" of Jesus to his readers. Rather than being simply a recycled philosophy or set of doctrines, this good news was unique—revolutionary, even—and sourced in the Son of God made flesh. Mark's emphasis to his readers is true for us today—the gospel of Jesus Christ, the Son of God, provides the hope we long for.

It's one thing to read about the story of Christianity. It's quite another to realize that it's *real*. Jesus walked on the earth. His best friends lived and died for his sake. Throughout history, men and women just like you have read the words of Mark.

You're part of that story. What you do with it, however, is up to you. When you finish today's reading, you'll close this book and leave it on a shelf or a table. But the story will continue—and you're a living, breathing part of it. What will you do today in light of that story? That good news? ∎

DAY FIVE

This week we've talked about Jesus as a victor. At this point you may be wondering why—why, since Mark doesn't call him that, are we calling Jesus a victor?

Let's do a bit of behind-the-scenes work.

PEEK AT THE GREEK εκβαλλω

In verse 12, Mark says that the Spirit "drove" Jesus into the wilderness. He uses the term *ekballo*, which means "force to leave." The word appears fifteen other times throughout Mark's gospel, most often in cases of exorcism where a demon is expelled. However, the idea here is not that Jesus was forced into the wilderness against his will, but rather that he went as a result of divine mandate, like the other uses of the term in Mark. In other words, Jesus went in obedience to the Father.

Way back in Genesis, in the beginning of the Bible, God makes a man and a woman and asks them to obey him. The Creator-God promises them everything: life, happiness, power, friendship, and rulership over all the earth. They just have to trust and obey.

They didn't.

Re-read Mark 1:11–13. Then, if you don't remember the story of Adam and Eve's failure, read Genesis 3:1–15 too.

[1] **What makes Jesus different? What makes him victorious, where Adam failed?**

We like to solve our own problems—to be the hero of our own story. But we don't always succeed. Take a few minutes here at the end of the week and write out your thoughts to God. If you need help getting started, consider this:

"I am unable to do _____, but you sent Jesus who could _____."

We love a good superhero. We want to *be* the superhero. But the truth is, we can't. God hasn't left us on our own, though. We have someone who's qualified. We have his story. Before we get farther down the road in Mark's gospel, we need to answer one question:

Will we follow Jesus? ∎

1

SYNAGOGUE IN CAPERNAUM

★ Jesus probably spoke in the synagogue in Capernaum as he called the first disciples, taught about the kingdom of God, and healed people.

SESSION 2:

Mark 1:14–45

We left last week's study with the question, "Will we follow Jesus?" So, how are you doing? Do you have an answer? This week, the passages in Mark we'll walk through will unpack one idea: True discipleship means following Jesus Christ. As his disciples, our goal isn't to hold one or two important doctrines or beliefs, but to surrender every aspect of our lives completely to Jesus.

By the end of this week, we want to accomplish three things:

- We want to understand that true discipleship requires a relationship with Jesus Christ.
- We want to feel motivated toward obedience by his love, not our guilt.
- We want to surrender every aspect of our lives to the Holy Spirit's transforming work.

As we go through this week's study in Mark, keep those objectives in mind.

WATCH: THE GOSPEL OF MARK WITH FRANCIS CHAN, SESSION 2

DAY ONE

In the last session, Francis showed us how the first thirteen verses give a pretty profound picture of Jesus's right to call people to follow him. And that's what Francis is excited about in this session—not only does Jesus have the right to call us, he does call us.

[14]Now after John was arrested, Jesus came into Galilee, proclaiming the gospel of God, [15]and saying, "The time is fulfilled, and the kingdom of God is at hand; repent and believe in the gospel."

[16]Passing alongside the Sea of Galilee, he saw Simon and Andrew the brother of Simon casting a net into the sea, for they were fishermen. [17]And Jesus said to them, "Follow me, and I will make you become fishers of men." [18]And immediately they left their nets and followed him. [19]And going on a little farther, he saw James the son of Zebedee and John his brother, who were in their boat mending the nets. [20]And immediately he called them, and they left their father Zebedee in the boat with the hired servants and followed him.

MARK 1:14–20

[1] How did you feel after watching the video? Spend some time reflecting on the picture that Francis painted of Jesus's authority and call.

The disciples weren't ideal choices for a rabbi's students. They were blue collar fishermen who knew little else except knot-tying and fish-gutting. But they leapt at the chance to follow this unusual rabbi when he called.

If we live comfortable lives, it's easy to see Jesus's call as an inconvenience. We have more to lose—more to give up—if we're going to follow him. **[2] Take some time and journal. What do you stand to lose by following Jesus the way the disciples did?** ∎

1

2

DAY TWO

Most of us have a mobile phone. Most of us can't live without it. Pretty much the entire world changed with the advent of a little computer brick we carry with us wherever we go.

But we're going to challenge that.

For the next fifteen minutes, try putting your phone down. Don't look at it. Better yet, turn it off entirely. Did you do it? Good.

Now let's look at the Gospel of Mark. Mark would have probably forgiven his audience for wondering just how unique Jesus really was. After all, most of them were Gentiles, and most of them had heard stories or myths of great heroes.

But in his gospel, Mark doesn't leave us wondering about the uniqueness of this Jesus. He makes sure we realize that this is the biggest moment in history. And he does it with one word—gospel.

Think back over your life. [1] **Describe a moment when life for you completely changed—where you knew the world was going to be different and there was no going back.**

1

All of us have life-changing moments in our personal histories. Maybe our view of the world changed when we realized there was no recess in middle school. Or maybe life transformed when we were in our first car accident.

Mark's doing something similar in this passage. Re-read chapter 1 and pay close attention to the reactions of the people to Jesus. Now think about your phone—have you been able to keep your mind off it so far?

We've gotten used to—addicted to, really—the life-altering technology of a mobile phone. But there was a time where it changed everything.

In a similar fashion, if we've been in the Christian world for any length of time, it's easy to forget that Jesus showing up on the scene was a huge deal. Just like people line up for the next iPhone, so too were people lining up to see Jesus.

Before ending today's study, take three more minutes (leave the phone off!) to talk to God. Ask that he open your eyes afresh to the life-altering reality of Jesus-come-to-earth. Then listen. Leave the rest of the time empty and listen to what God brings to your mind. **² Finally, write anything that stands out to you through today's study. ▪**

2

The remains of the Capernaum Synagogue are not from the synagogue in Jesus's day. The style of architecture and design elements, along with archeological evidence, suggests the remains standing today are from the Roman era in the 2nd or 3rd century AD. The common conclusion among scholars is the remains of the synagogue during Jesus's time form the foundation of the one standing today.

DAY THREE

We've already established in Mark 1:15 that Jesus came into this world to proclaim the kingdom of God. His earthly presence signaled that God was done preparing. But what is the kingdom of God, exactly?

During the time of Jesus, the Jewish community anticipated a militaristic kingdom where God would rule over the nations through Israel. However, Jesus flipped that idea on its head. In his gospel, Mark uses the expression "kingdom of God" fourteen times.

From the start, in 1:15, Jesus says, "the kingdom of God is at hand." The verb he uses literally means "has drawn near," and he immediately ties it to repentance and belief. Not once does Mark refer to "the kingdom of God" in terms of an outward militaristic kingdom, like the one anticipated by the Jews. Rather, Jesus declares that the reign of God begins with the internal surrender of his people.

In other words, we are no longer waiting. The kingdom of God is spreading even now, and it takes root primarily in the hearts of people. It's easy for us to get caught up in thinking similar to that of the Jews during Jesus's time. They longed for power, and we do the same today. We talk a lot about Christianity's influence in culture. While there's nothing wrong with that, we have to remember that the kingdom of God begins first and foremost with a transformed heart.

God is at work creating a people, which means the focus of discipleship is helping people surrender to and follow Jesus. Jesus did not come simply to change our circumstances but to transform our hearts. Think of the people left waiting for Jesus to heal them when, in Mark 1:35–38, he leaves for other towns. If all they came to Jesus for was physical healing, then they were surely disappointed.

[1] **So, what do you come to Jesus looking for? Write out an honest prayer to him, confessing wrongheaded expectations of Jesus, and asking for a desire to surrender and follow.** ■

1

DAY FOUR

In the first twenty verses, we've seen Jesus declare his purpose: to announce the kingdom of God and call people into it. In Mark 1:21, Jesus begins to demonstrate his purpose through miraculous works.

Read Mark 1:21–34.

Throughout the video, Francis emphasized the authority of Jesus as a driving factor for discipleship. [1] **So, let's take a moment to observe and list all the ways that Mark highlights Jesus's authority. Pay special attention to which people Jesus helps with his authority.**

These verses give us the first glimpses of Jesus's power on display. He does not just claim to have authority— he proves it. His authority reaches over both the physical and the spiritual realms. Mark makes it clear that those oppressed by demons were not simply dealing with psychological disorders (1:32). Because of that, Jesus casting out demons illustrates, in a very practical way, the kingdom of God replacing that of Satan in the world.

Even more, Jesus extends the benefits of his authority to unlikely people. During biblical times, women were considered less-than, so much so that their testimony was not considered legitimate in a court of law. But Jesus goes out of his way to heal Peter's mother-in-law. He goes out of his way to heal a leper—someone no self-respecting Jew would go anywhere near.

1

THE GOSPEL OF MARK

The point Mark's driving at with this presentation of Jesus's authority is that he has the right to extend the kingdom to whomever he chooses. And that includes the sick, marginalized, and hurting.

So what does this mean for us? How do we live differently in light of Jesus's authority?

Well, if we're Christians, it means Jesus alone has the right to extend the kingdom to people. And we should never ignore or deny those to whom he's offered citizenship.

² Think of one person who grates on you—the last person in the world you'd want Jesus to offer the kingdom to. Why do you feel that way? What would have to change in your attitude in order to treat that person the way Jesus demonstrates in our passage this week?

As we've said before, Jesus is our savior and our model for obedience. He is both our guide for what it looks like to follow God faithfully and the one who enables us to do so. A lot has changed since biblical times, but our human nature remains the same. Confess your struggles to God and ask him to give you a heart to see people the way he does.■

2

> " ...he's calling people to himself and he's coming with this authority, saying, 'Follow me. The kingdom of heaven—this is something completely new.' "

DAY FIVE

Following Jesus is a work in progress.
That's what discipleship is all about.
That remains true for us today just as
it did with the very first disciples.

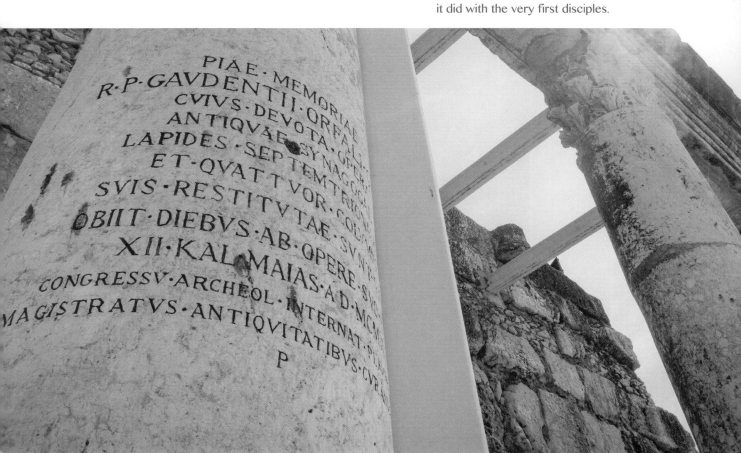

If you remember back to Francis's teaching, he concluded by saying he hopes we understand what authority Jesus has to ask us to follow him. When we encounter Jesus, our response should be, "I'll do anything to follow this man."

But sometimes, our reasons for following might not be quite right.

Re-read Mark 1:35–45.

PEEK AT THE GREEK καταδιωκω

Like Francis pointed out in the video, it didn't take long for Jesus's popularity to gain traction. Yet, after attracting one of his first crowds (1:33) he steals away in solitude to pray (1:35). Confused by his withdrawal, the disciples "searched for him" (1:36). Interestingly, Mark uses the verb *katadioko*, which nearly always describes a hostile form of pursuit—like a bounty hunter chasing an escaped prisoner. The disciples are looking for Jesus because they feel like he's blowing the opportunity to capitalize on his growing fame. Instead, they find him praying in solitude. By using the verb *katadioko*, Mark suggests their misplaced craving for influence through Jesus, which is fundamentally a misunderstanding of the purposes of God.

[1] **Jesus's response to his own fame differs from his disciples' response. Being honest, how do you think you would have responded to Jesus?**

1

Jesus may have been going first-century viral, but he stayed focused on the Father no matter the cost. In Mark 1:35–39, Jesus remains committed to the Father's will through prayer and by moving on to other towns to preach. Even if we never experience the kind of popularity Jesus did, it's easy for us to drift into distraction and lose sight of God's will.

2 Describe some of the distractions that divert your attention from the Father. How do they affect your willingness to obey him?

3 Pick one distraction. Maybe it's your phone like the experiment we did earlier this week. Whatever you choose, commit to setting it aside until next week. Take a moment now to ask God what he'd like to do with the time instead.

We are prone to acting like the disciples, more concerned about what we'll get out of the arrangement than doing the Father's will. Participating in kingdom work does not mean fitting Jesus into our schedule. It means submitting our lives to his call whenever and wherever it leads. ∎

2

3

Our career, our family,

everything else—we've got

to understand they are so

low compared to the calling

of Jesus.

CAPERNAUM & SHORES OF GALILEE

★ Capernaum was the closest thing Jesus had to a "home base" throughout his ministry, likely chosen because his earliest disciples (Peter and Andrew) lived there.

SESSION 3:

Mark 2:1–3:6

Last week we laid down the challenge to follow Jesus with our whole lives—surrendering our time, our comfort, and our expectations. But that's not the whole story. Something sinister stands in our way—something we didn't necessarily put there but have to deal with if we want to follow Jesus.

The main thing we're looking at this week is simple: Jesus is looking for those who recognize their sin.

- We want to understand that only Jesus offers the relief all of humanity longs for.
- We want to feel genuine relief through the forgiveness Jesus offers.
- We want to begin to obey as a result of Jesus's forgiveness.

As always, as we go through this week's study in Mark, keep those objectives in mind.

WATCH: THE GOSPEL OF MARK WITH FRANCIS CHAN, SESSION 3

DAY ONE

1

2

¹And when he returned to Capernaum after some days, it was reported that he was at home. ²And many were gathered together, so that there was no more room, not even at the door. And he was preaching the word to them. ³And they came, bringing to him a paralytic carried by four men. ⁴And when they could not get near him because of the crowd, they removed the roof above him, and when they had made an opening, they let down the bed on which the paralytic lay. ⁵And when Jesus saw their faith, he said to the paralytic, "Son, your sins are forgiven." ⁶Now some of the scribes were sitting there, questioning in their hearts, ⁷"Why does this man speak like that? He is blaspheming! Who can forgive sins but God alone?" ⁸And immediately Jesus, perceiving in his spirit that they thus questioned within themselves, said to them, "Why do you question these things in your hearts? ⁹Which is easier, to say to the paralytic, 'Your sins are forgiven,' or to say, 'Rise, take up your bed and walk'? ¹⁰But that you may know that the Son of Man has authority on earth to forgive sins"—he said to the paralytic— ¹¹"I say to you, rise, pick up your bed, and go home." ¹²And he rose and immediately picked up his bed and went out before them all, so that they were all amazed and glorified God, saying, "We never saw anything like this!"

MARK 2:1–12

Throughout the first chapter, Francis returned to the central idea of Jesus's authority. Jesus proves with his words and actions that he is more than a gifted man. He has a unique claim—a claim to the very authority and power of God himself.

Francis relayed the story of the paralytic whom Jesus healed. If you need a refresher, look in Mark 2:1–12. Thanks to the stories in chapter 1, we already saw Jesus heal just about every kind of problem. This vignette narrows the camera shot, if you will, to something more important behind the healings.

¹Take a moment and think about the things in your life you'd like Jesus to fix. If he showed up one day and said, "Name it and I'll fix it," what would you ask from him? Why?

We expect Jesus to offer here in chapter 2 what he's been offering the whole way through chapter 1: healing—fixing the people's problems. And Jesus does that here, but not in the way we've come to expect.

Put yourself in the shoes of someone inside that house with Jesus. You're surrounded by everyday people as well as Jewish officials and teachers listening to Jesus talk about his Father's kingdom.

²What would you—along with the people in the house—expect from Jesus when the paralytic comes down through a hole in the roof?

Mark pulls us as the readers in along with everyone else in that room. Because we've seen Jesus work wonders in chapter 1, we expect the same here. But that's not what we get. Instead, Jesus addresses the young man's sin.

Francis described the scene as Jesus's "boldest statement so far." The effects are immediate—the gathered Jewish scholars and officials would have hit the roof if there wasn't already a hole in it. Sin was the great barrier between God and humanity and here was Jesus saying he could deal with that problem.

[3] **If you're being honest, how big of a deal is your sin? Look back at the things you wrote you'd like Jesus to fix. Where do they rank compared to the sin that separates you from God?**

For the Jewish leaders, miraculous healing in the name of God's kingdom was one thing. But forgiveness? That was one step too far. Jesus doesn't let the issue rest, though. He straight up challenges the people's conceptions of what their problem really was. A disabled body was the symptom of a world stained by sin. Jesus had come to do battle with the real problem.

Now read Mark 2:13–17. Here, Mark fast-forwards the scene right after to the moment where Jesus called the disciple we know as Matthew—the author of the first gospel. Once again, the religious leaders lose it at the thought that this prophet-like man would dine with sinners. But they'd forgotten the lesson already—Jesus was here to deal with that sin. As with the paralytic's sickness, he could heal sin too.

This week's study in Mark is going to challenge us to wrestle with the realities of our sinfulness and our deep need for Jesus. We cannot fix ourselves any more than the paralytic could stand on his own. We need a daring rescue from the kingdom of darkness.

But there's good news. Jesus has come, and the kingdom of light follows in his footsteps. ▪

3

"

There's a bigger thing

you've got to understand:

You're standing before a

holy God, and Jesus can

make peace for you. He can

forgive everything you've

ever done.

"

DAY TWO

Yesterday, Mark introduced us as his readers to the archenemy of Jesus in the gospel: sin. We saw Jesus demonstrate his fearless approach in dealing with the one thing that separates humanity from our Creator.

But some people didn't think it was that simple.

Chapter 2 gives us our first look at those who would begin to oppose the ministry of Jesus. Verse 6 mentions the "scribes" who considered Jesus's words blasphemous. These "scribes" have been mentioned once previously (1:22). They were religious scholars and experts when it came to interpreting rabbinic law.

Later, verse 16 introduces the Pharisees, who were a group of separatists distinguished by their stringent adherence to rabbinic law. They "separated" themselves by refusing to keep company with "sinners," like those mentioned in the rest of Mark 2. And while scribes could also be Pharisees, few Pharisees were in fact scribes.

Both groups, however, knew the Scriptures backward and forward. They devoted their lives to the very words of God, yet failed to recognize God-in-the-flesh. Even worse, they also accused him of blasphemy (2:7) and plotted his death (3:6). Clearly being an expert in the things of God doesn't mean we actually know him.

Today we have more access than ever to information. With the internet and smartphones, the Bible is at our fingertips at all times. And yet we so quickly forget that, fundamentally, we're sinners in need of a healer.

[1]**Take the next five minutes and spend some time praying. Confess your sins to Jesus. Admit your need for him. Ask him to reveal to you the sins that you're ignoring or forgetting. And then listen. Allow him the time to work in your heart and mind.** ∎

DAY THREE

This week, we've been looking at the problem of sin as Mark presents it in his gospel. Different groups of people react differently to Jesus's handling of sin: the people who recognize their sinfulness repent and follow him. The people who just want something out of Jesus look for miracles. And the people whose authority Jesus's words undercut are getting madder.

In the last half of chapter 2, we find two somewhat strange vignettes. We're going to take a closer look. Grab your Bible and read Mark 2:18–3:6. As you read, look for a few different things:

[1] **First, what's the focus of Jesus's ministry? People or theological correctness?**

[2] **Second, who benefits from what Jesus says? Who loses out?**

[3] **Finally, what do Jesus's words tell you about how God treats his people?**

These passages are tricky. The wineskins and heads of grain feel a little lost-in-translation. But if we focus instead on what Jesus's words and actions mean for the people who heard them originally, we'll find something important.

Look back at your observations. Did you notice that Jesus's response to the Pharisees encourages celebration and health for his disciples? Jesus makes the point that, in everyday life, we do what's appropriate for any given situation—whether it's fixing a worn-out pair of pants or keeping food from spoiling or eating so we don't starve or healing the sick.

When those who follow Jesus recognize their sin and Jesus's ability to destroy it, they're able to follow him into the kingdom of God. And that kingdom brings celebration and provision. As the king, Jesus can and does provide for his followers. In doing so, Jesus also proves that God wanted to do that from the beginning.

For example, what the Pharisees turned into a burdensome ritual (prohibiting work on the Sabbath), Jesus returned to God's original intent—rest and provision for his people. Francis described Jesus's actions as not just talking about but also showing the nature of God's kingdom.

So, what does this have to do with how we live our lives? Too often, we come at our relationship with God like the Pharisees and scribes—like it's a transaction. We hold up our end of the deal, and God's obligated to hold up his. But in today's passage, we've seen that God provides for his people not because they're obedient but because they come to and follow Jesus.

[4] **Take some time and think about how you approach your relationship with God. Do you gravitate towards transactions—checking off a list to be on God's good side? What would your life look like if, instead, you chose to follow Jesus first and foremost, and trusted God to provide for the rest? What's stopping you from making that choice?**

As you work through these questions, do so prayerfully. Ask God to instill in you the courage to follow Jesus and trust him for the rest. ∎

4

"

Jesus explains, 'Look,

this is who I came for. I

came for those who are sick.'

That's what a physician

does. He doesn't come for

the healthy.

"

DAY FOUR

We've been wrestling with some hard things so far. It's never fun or easy to look our sin in the eye. It's more than a little terrifying to pull it out of the dark recesses of our hearts and put it out there for Jesus to deal with.

Today, we're going to look at one of the hard truths of the human heart—we can wall ourselves off from God for very different reasons and still end up at the same place.

Take a minute and re-read Mark 3:1–6, especially verse 5. Then, turn over to the Old Testament and look at Ezekiel 11:17–21.

The parallels between the two passages may not jump out right away. Ezekiel's addressing the nation of Israel after God had punished her for rebelling against him. They'd fallen into deep depravity and completely stopped following his laws. As a result, he'd sent them into exile.

Ezekiel's prophecy, however, points to a day when God's people would return to the land of Israel and he would fundamentally change their hearts—from hard stone to soft flesh. As a result, instead of disobeying his law, they would follow it happily.

As he writes his gospel, Mark knows about the tendency in God's people to harden their hearts against him. But here's the irony—the religious leaders had become so obsessed with following God's law (what's promised in Ezekiel) that their hearts were hardened against Jesus and his desire to do God's will.

One group's heart is hard because they want to disobey, the other group's heart is hard because they think they are obeying. The problem, however, isn't the obedience or disobedience at all—the problem's the heart. Whether we're talking about the exiles in Ezekiel or the Pharisees in Mark or us today, we all want to control our lives. We want to have the last word on what happens in and around us.

For the exiles, that meant chasing paganism. For the Pharisees, that meant obligating God through religious fervor. What does it look like for you?

[1] **Spend some time alone—just you and God—and do a bit of journaling. Write out the areas of your life where you tend to fight God for control. Then ask yourself why: Why do you want to keep God out? Finally, think about what you might be missing as a result of hardening yourself to God.**

Jesus's ministry wasn't about miraculous healings for their own sake. He was proving his ability to restore what sin destroyed. Through him, we have the opportunity to live in right relationship with God. But that means letting go of control. ▪

1

DAY FIVE

This week's chunk of Mark ends on a depressing note. Despite witnessing God-in-the-flesh and hearing the very teachings of the promised deliverer, the religious leaders respond by plotting to kill Jesus. Throughout our passage, we see a clear escalation. What began as antagonistic questioning (2:16) grew into a murderous rage (3:6)—one that'll end in a crucifixion.

PEEK AT THE GREEK *απολλυμι*

When talking about the Pharisees' desire to kill Jesus, Mark uses the term *apollumi*, which in this context means, "to ruin" or "destroy." It's a word without sympathy, often used in the New Testament to describe the destruction of sinners (Mark 12:9; Luke 17:27, 29; Jude 5). Considering the previous verses, it's also deeply ironic. Jesus cast out a demon (1:21–28), healed and forgave a paralytic (2:1–12), communicated the correct use of Old Testament law (2:18–28), and restored a man's withered hand (3:1–5). Despite all of this, the Pharisees sought to kill him, the one who came to bring life where death had formerly reigned.

No one reaches the point of outrightly rejecting God overnight. Francis left this week's video session asking us to consider the trajectory of our lives. The hopeful truth is that we don't have to end up hardened.

Jesus demands a decision, yes. And yes, he leaves no room for ambivalence—we are either with him or we oppose him. There is no in-between. Jesus is looking for followers who recognize their sin, submit to his authority, and follow him into life.

We've had a chance to do that this week. We've looked at the sin in our lives and confessed it to God. We've looked at the areas where we fight God for control and worked to surrender those to him.

But as we saw with the paralytic, the disciples, and the man with the withered hand, Jesus offers life too. He expects us to offer him all of our lives and in return he offers us all of his life.

In a moment, you'll put this book down. Maybe you'll start your last day of work for the week, or you'll close your eyes to sleep before the weekend starts. You'll go on living your life.

As you do, take this thought with you: Jesus has come to offer you life. Will you follow him into it? ▪

BETHSAIDA &
SEA OF GALILEE

⭐ Bethsaida is one of the three towns in Galilee mentioned by name in the Gospels. It was the hometown of Peter, Andrew, and Philip.

SESSION 4:

Mark 3:7–4:34

In the last three weeks, we've looked at what it takes to start following Jesus on the road of discipleship. We've accepted the authority of Jesus and acknowledged our sin. We've taken that step out into the vulnerable territory of submitting to his leadership in every area of our life.

As we return to Mark this week, we'll start getting an idea of what it looks like to actually walk on the road that Jesus leads us down. Scripture never promises an easy time following Jesus, but it does make it clear that exchanging obedience to the savior for worldly comfort is a cheap trade.

Through this week's study, we want to accomplish three things:

- We want to recognize that discipleship is about advancing the kingdom of God.
- We want to feel confidence in our acceptance through Jesus.
- And we want to work at bearing fruit in keeping with our discipleship.

As we go through this week's study in Mark, keep those objectives in mind.

WATCH: THE GOSPEL OF MARK WITH FRANCIS CHAN, SESSION 4

DAY ONE

When we think about Jesus, we often picture a kind-faced man who welcomes everyone. Sure the religious leaders didn't like him, but everyone else was on his side, right?

As we keep trekking through Mark, we're going to find not two reactions to Jesus but three—three groups that respond to the savior in different ways. In the video session, Francis pointed out that Jesus's plan all along was to focus not on the impressive crowds but on the twelve disciples.

We could make a big deal about the suitability of the disciples but take a closer look at Mark 3:7–19. [1] **What sets the disciples apart from the crowds following Jesus?**

If we commit our lives to following Jesus, it can be easy to fall into a way of living that treats Jesus as an add-on. We live our lives, and when it's convenient, we'll go to church or read our Bible.

But Francis pointed out that Jesus's plan was to build into twelve young people. They'd started following him, yes, but Jesus chose them to be part of his intense discipleship program that would end in his death in Jerusalem.

Discipleship is no "add-on" program. It's not something you can have in addition to the rest of your life's pursuits. Francis summarized Jesus's message in chapter 4 by saying, "You want to follow Jesus? You have to give everything up."

[2] **Think about that for a second. If you were to pursue true discipleship, what would you stand to lose? Are you okay with that?**

1

2

The challenge of Jesus's road of discipleship lies primarily in what it costs us. Success in Jesus's mind is completely different than success by the world's standards. We have to live in this world, yes, but to be a disciple of Jesus means prioritizing his call over everything—even family, as Jesus points out in Mark 3:31–35.

[3] **Take a minute or two and think about how Francis presented the two groups of people: the called-out disciples and the crowds. If you were to look at your life honestly, which group would you belong to?**

[4] **What's one thing this week you can begin to surrender to Jesus in order to better embrace the call of discipleship?**

Jesus has offered the invitation of discipleship to each of us, but it's a costly journey. When he calls, what will you answer? ■

3

4

DAY TWO

1

2

Today we're going to dig a little bit deeper into the text of Mark 3:7–35. So, grab your Bible, open it up, and let's get going. In our passage, Mark's doing some interesting things. He's playing with two main themes but splits them up across four main sections of text. Those four are Mark 3:7–12, 13–21, 22–30, and 31–35.

¹ Take a few minutes and read each of those passages. Then, write out the similarities you notice between 3:7–12 and 22–30, as well as between 3:13–21 and 31–35. If you need a bit of help, ask yourself who the main characters are in each vignette apart from Jesus.

Mark bounces from the theme of Jesus and demons to Jesus and his true family and back again. The four stories together form a whole, all driving at one main idea. In the first section (3:7–12), the very demons Jesus casts out validate his identity and his mission. In the third section (3:22–30), the scribes attempt to invalidate Jesus's ministry by saying he does his miracles by Satan.

² What's the irony in the way those two passages work together? What do you think Mark is trying to say about the scribes?

In the middle of the sections featuring demons, Mark includes two vignettes about Jesus's family. In the second of the four sections (3:13–21), Jesus essentially selects twelve new family members, while his biological family thinks he's lost his mind. In the final section (3:31–35), Jesus categorically rejects the claim his biological family may make on him to reestablish the "new" family he's creating.

[3] **Based on how Mark's paired these two vignettes together, what can we conclude about the nature of Jesus's true family? How do or should they view Jesus?**

In all four sections, Jesus's purpose on earth has a polarizing effect. For the scribes and the biological family of Jesus, his actions seem insane— demonic even. But for the disciples and the demons themselves, Jesus is far, far more.

We've talked a lot about the high cost of discipleship last week and this week. But today's study comes with a significant warning—be careful in dismissing Jesus. Now, most of us don't set out to just attribute the work of Jesus to demons like the scribes did. And most of us won't call him insane.

But Jesus has placed a demanding call on each of us. When that demand runs up against our expectations for how our lives should go, we have a choice to make—do the will of the Father and follow Jesus, or dismiss him. Which will you make today? ■

3

"

Nowadays, we would look at Jesus as such a failure, spending his whole life with a dozen guys. And that's all he has to show for the end of his life. Yet, when you think about it, his plan was, 'Let me build into these guys' lives. And when I'm done, they're the ones that are going to carry it on.'

"

DAY THREE

One of the beauties of studying a book of the Bible from beginning to end is that it keeps verses in context. We have to read each passage in light of what's going on around it. However, this kind of study also makes it impossible to avoid the harder portions of the Bible, like the one we find in Mark 3:22–30. It's one of the more difficult teachings from Jesus—the so-called unforgiveable sin.

In the passage, the scribes confront Jesus about his teachings. They've begun to spread the rumor that he is possessed by a demon named "Beelzebul," which was a high-ranking deity worshiped in Canaanite religion. Jesus easily points out the flaw in their logic, however. If Jesus worked for Satan, why would he cast out demons that also work for Satan? He would be fighting against his own cause.

But then Jesus utters a frightening statement: "But whoever blasphemes against the Holy Spirit never has forgiveness, but is guilty of an eternal sin" (3:29). Clearly, it's a warning, but what does it mean? And how can we know whether or not we are guilty of such a terrible sin?

Remember back to last week where we discussed the idea of trajectory. The religious leaders didn't simply wake up one morning and decide to oppose Jesus. Their hearts hardened over time through a series of small decisions that calloused them to the truth. We're seeing the end result of that here. The scribes have arrived at such a hard-hearted state they are willing to attribute the miraculous works of Jesus to Satan rather than the Holy Spirit. Jesus is making it clear that his works are possible because of the Holy Spirit in contrast to the power of Satan.

It's also important to note the verb in Mark 3:30. Most translations say "they were saying" and, while that's accurate, the verb's tense in Greek implies an action that occurred on a habitual basis. In other words, this wasn't a one-time event. The scribes regularly and continually attributed the works of the Holy Spirit through Jesus to the power of Satan, which is what Jesus declares unforgivable.

Despite the seriousness of Jesus's accusation, we should not miss the hope in Jesus's words before his warning: Jesus says, "all sins will be forgiven" along with "whatever blasphemies" when we turn to him. But someone who's made a habit of declaring Jesus a servant of Satan demonstrates his or her refusal to turn to Jesus in repentance.

So, if you're worried about whether or not you've committed the unforgivable sin, you can be sure already that you haven't committed it. Your heart is sensitive to the conviction of the Holy Spirit, and you're chasing Jesus. All the other sins you may have piled up in your life are forgiven in him.

Take the next five minutes and spend some time praying. Thank the Father that, through Jesus, you have complete forgiveness. Then ask the Holy Spirit to continue to prick your conscience over sins in your life so that you never develop a trajectory toward hardness. ∎

1

DAY FOUR

We're moving into chapter 4 of Mark today, and we're going to find one of the most interesting kinds of teaching we get from Jesus—parables. In the video session, Francis pointed out that Jesus intentionally taught in parables to limit his audience. The massive crowds that followed Jesus for what he could do for them would miss the point, but the disciples who'd given up everything for Jesus would get it.

Since Mark includes Jesus's explanations in chapter 4, he intends us to also get it. So, let's look at the text. Read Mark 4:1–20. The Parable of the Sower is one of Jesus's most famous parables for good reason. It lays out the path of true discipleship for us along with all the possible pitfalls along the road.

If you've been around church for long, chances are pretty good you've heard this parable used as a sort of barometer to tell whether someone's a Christian or not. But that's not really what Jesus is trying to get at.

Remember, the message of Mark is the road of discipleship. So far, we've seen barriers (sin) and warnings (hardened hearts) when it comes to discipleship. But now Jesus sits down in a boat and explains what the journey actually looks like.

Think about the four soils. If you're a believer—or even just starting out learning about Jesus—chances are you're not the first soil where the call to discipleship never takes root. But even if we don't fit the first category, that doesn't mean we automatically fit the last one.

[1]**Take a moment and do some journaling. For each of the three kinds of soils after the first, reflect on your spiritual journey. Describe those times in your life where your faithful following of Jesus struggled to take root. Unpack the particular cares of the world that've threatened to strangle your role as disciple in Jesus. Finally, celebrate those moments where you've seen success.** ∎

1

DAY FIVE

As we wrap up this week's study in chapters 3 and 4 of Mark, we're going to take a moment to consider the scope of what discipleship is all about. Think back to the scene that Mark has painted for us so far: Massive crowds have been following Jesus. He's drawn attention from nearly everyone—including his own mother and brothers.

Now put yourself in the shoes of the disciples, watching this whole thing unfold. Sure, Jesus has been talking in parables to keep the mysteries of God's kingdom hidden from the masses, but still—this new kingdom Jesus has been talking about looks well underway. Doesn't it?

We live in an era—particularly in the United States—where we've come to expect our lives to make a big impact. Our professions, our talents, our churches. We want it all to make a difference in the world.

In the last three, short parables in our chunk of text for this week, Jesus paints a slightly different picture of success. Take a minute and read through Mark 4:21–34. As you do, consider what Jesus is saying about the way the kingdom grows.

It's easy to fall into the habit of thinking that the goal of our discipleship is to change the world. And Jesus's description of the growth of the kingdom is definitely world-changing. But notice what Jesus likens each of his disciples to: not the whole city, not the whole harvest, and not the whole tree.

Instead, the kingdom grows with the small contributions of many parts: a single lamp, a single grain, or a single mustard seed.

[1] **If you were honest with yourself, would you describe your life as world-changing? Why or why not?**

Jesus calls us onto the road of discipleship in order to grow the kingdom of God. And that kingdom will, ultimately, change the world. But our contributions are likely to be small—hardly noticeable. And that's okay, because it's the kingdom that matters—not our fame.

So as we wrap up this week, ponder this question: [2] **Will you continue to follow Jesus even if it means a lifetime of obscurity?**

The promise Jesus offers is, in the end, a huge kingdom built by God himself. We have the opportunity to play a small part in building it. Is that enough for you? ∎

1

2

SEA
OF
GALILEE

05

SESSION 5:

Mark 4:35–5:43

Our study in Mark has led us into some challenging questions so far. Jesus has laid down the challenge of discipleship—not just for the twelve disciples, but for us too. In the past few weeks, we've seen just how demanding the call to follow Jesus can be.

But this week, we're going to get a glimpse of the kindness of the one we follow. We live in a fallen world. We will experience times of pain and suffering. But our hope is in the presence of the savior.

As a result of this week's study, we want to accomplish three things:

- We want to know with confidence that Jesus is present with us in every circumstance.
- We want to feel gratitude for the transformation God has brought about in our lives.
- And we want to face our fears with the faith that God is our refuge.

As we go through this week's study in Mark, keep those objectives in mind.

WATCH: THE GOSPEL OF MARK WITH FRANCIS CHAN, SESSION 5

DAY ONE

Have you ever taken a gamble on something? Maybe it was something as simple as attempting a different route home from work when an accident shuts down the highway. Or perhaps you had to take a bigger risk in navigating a particularly tricky relationship.

Regardless of how you've experienced it, you're probably familiar with the crushing anxiety that comes with waiting to find out if a bet would pay off. As we look at our next section of the Gospel of Mark, we're going to experience alongside the disciples that same kind of anxiety. But we're also going to see Jesus step into that worry and offer confident hope.

So, grab your Bible and open it to Mark 4:35–41. We left off the story with Jesus explaining the nature of God's kingdom to his disciples: It was a kingdom that, though it starts small, would grow into a world-changing endeavor.

Right after, Jesus and his disciples decide to go on a day trip across the Sea of Galilee. Read Mark 4:35–41. In the video session, Francis taught from a boat on that very sea.

[1] **Put yourself in the shoes of the disciples. What do you think it would have been like to experience the storm now that you've seen the sea itself?**

1

Before we jump to judge the disciples for their fear, we have to remember that these are seasoned fishermen. They know the power of sea storms. They aren't afraid because they've never seen choppy water before.

In the same way, we experience fear in the course of our everyday lives that's well-founded. As we walk the road of discipleship, we have to recognize that Jesus sees and acknowledges the reality of our fears.

[2] **Take a minute or two and reflect back on a time in your life where a situation or set of circumstances left you feeling afraid. In the midst of that fear, what did your perspective of God look like?**

It says something important about the disciples that, instead of dealing with the source of their problem directly, they turned to Jesus. They'd seen him perform miracle after miracle. They knew he could save them. But their fear came from doubting whether he would save them.

In the midst of that fear, Jesus displays his power in the grandest way yet. On seeing the way in which Jesus saved them, the disciples' fear moves from the sea to Jesus himself. He's far more than they ever imagined.

Spend the next few minutes praying. Ask God to open your eyes to his true nature. Ask him to point out and remove the false beliefs you have about who he is and what he wants to do in your life. And then thank him that he is with you in the midst of the storm. ∎

2

DAY TWO

1

We started this week's discussion by thinking about a time where we weren't sure if something we'd banked on was going to pay off. The road of discipleship can feel that way sometimes. The twelve disciples, for instance, had left their livelihoods to follow Jesus. They'd banked everything on him, and the road in front of them wasn't looking easy.

We've already seen their fear show up when facing down a storm at sea. Jesus proved not only his ability to save his followers, but also his power. Today, we're going to see Jesus go toe-to-toe with a different kind of storm. The story of the demon-possessed man comes right after the disciples see Jesus's awe-inspiring display of power on the sea. Mark wants to make sure we have that in the back of our minds as Jesus encounters a storm—but this time it's on the inside of a person.

Read Mark 5:1–20. As you read, look for parallels between the storm on the Sea of Galilee and the horde of demons in the man from Gerasenes.

[1] **What did you notice was similar between the two vignettes? What was different?**

Just as the storm, wind, and waves fell immediately silent at the voice of Jesus, so also here do the demons possessing the poor man recognize Jesus. In fact, the parallels go deep into the original language.

PEEK AT THE GREEK επετιμησεν | πεφιμωσο

The account of Jesus calming the storm is one of his most famous miracles in all of the Gospels. However, some of the terminology Mark uses to describe the scene parallels a previous miracle. Mark 4:39 says that Jesus "rebuked" (*epitemesen*) the wind and commanded the sea to "be still" (*pephimoso*). The exact same terms appear back in Mark 1:25 when Jesus heals the man possessed by a demonic spirit, which may imply some sort of evil presence magnifying the terror of the storm described here. Mark frames the calming of the storm like an exorcism. Jesus speaks to the elements and they listen. The term translated "be still" can also literally read, "be muzzled" (1 Cor. 9:9; 1 Tim. 5:18), as though the weather were a disobedient animal forced to submit to the command of its owner.

Take a look at verse 15 again. After Jesus permits the demons to drive a herd of pigs into the sea (the same sea Jesus had conquered a few verses before), the townspeople see and are afraid. They respond in the same way the disciples did in the boat—the raw power of Jesus is, frankly, stunning.

By pairing yesterday's passage with today's, Mark wants his readers to come away with a very powerful picture of Jesus. No matter how hopeless or overwhelming our experience on the road of discipleship is, Jesus is with us. That should encourage us immensely.

Before we end our study of Mark 5:1–20, notice one final thing: once the man is free of the demons, he immediately wants to follow Jesus. He wants to be a disciple. But instead, Jesus sends him home—not because Jesus doesn't want the man with him, but so that he can be a missionary to his town.

When we see God's power on display in our lives, it can (and should) motivate us to tell others about the God we serve. He is with us. He works on our behalf. Will you tell others?

[2] Take a few minutes and write out a story of when you saw God do something powerful on your behalf. Maybe, like the disciples on the sea, it was something *for* you. Or maybe, like the demon-possessed man, it was something *in* you. Write it down, and, if you have the opportunity, tell someone the story today. ▪

2

"

If there's still fear in

your life, it's because

you don't really

believe that he's there.

"

DAY THREE

Before we get to the rest of this week's passage, we're going to stop and look at one of the more bizarre parts of the story from yesterday. What's the deal with the pigs? Other than the pigs, Jesus only destroys something with his power one other time (Mark 11:12–14, 20–21). So, what do we make of it?

From the start, we should acknowledge that there are cultural differences between us and first-century Israel. Jews didn't raise pigs as livestock because they were ritually unclean. But Gentiles did. Herds like the one in Mark 5:1–20 were a source of income. Jesus doesn't actually command the demons to inhabit or kill the pigs, but he does give them permission.

The dramatic end to the demons' power displays Jesus's ability to totally dominate demonic activity. Previously, the possessed man lived in a cemetery, broke every form of restraint placed on him, and walked around naked, cutting himself with stones and screaming at nearby residents. At the command of Jesus, all of that changed. The demons departed, and he sat down calmly before Jesus.

1

Yet how do the people from the city respond? "They began to beg Jesus to depart from the region" (5:17). Jesus had freed a man of a legion of demons. But the townsfolk cared only that the freedom had cost them their livestock. Rather than praise Jesus for what he had done, they were terrified by his power and cared more for their pigs than they did for this man now free from demonic oppression.

Now, most of us aren't pig farmers. Following Jesus probably won't mean a complete collapse of our agricultural enterprise. But following Jesus does come with a cost. The salvation he offers means depending wholly on him instead of on what we've come to trust for safety—financial or otherwise.

[1] **As you go through your day today, think about the small things you've come to rely on to get through the day—your morning coffee, your car, or a motivational social media account. What would happen if, in order for you to be able to follow Jesus fully, those things disappeared?**

Would you, like the townsfolk, turn on Jesus? Or would you, like the demon-possessed man, turn to Jesus?

It's a question only you can answer. ∎

DAY FOUR

1

2

We've been following the disciples' journey so far in our study of Mark. But today we're going to look at another unlikely follower of Jesus. Just as the disciples put it all on the line to chase Jesus, so too will she risk everything.

Open your Bible to Mark 5:21–34. As you read the text, think about how the woman's perspective of Jesus differs from the disciples' reaction in the boat.

So, after healing the demon-possessed man, Jesus returns to the other side of the sea and immediately gets swarmed. But in the middle of that swarm is a synagogue ruler whose daughter is dying. Jesus consents to go with him in order to heal the girl, but along the way something unique happens.

[1] What did you notice about the woman's attitude toward Jesus? How would you compare her confidence in him to the way the disciples viewed Jesus on the sea?

The woman had already spent her life's savings on cures for her condition. She'd bet the farm on the doctors and they'd failed her. But she had heard about Jesus. Like the disciples, she knew what Jesus had done for others, and she hoped he'd be there for her too.

But when she touched Jesus's robes, not only was she healed, but Jesus also noticed. The disciples thought he was being silly, but Jesus knew someone had approached him in faith.

[2] Look at verses 32–33. How did the woman's approach to Jesus resemble those of the disciples in the storm or the townspeople from across the sea?

It makes perfect sense to fear power. When something completely outstrips our comprehension, we typically start shaking in our boots. But the woman approaches Jesus out of fear of what he might say about her—being unclean—touching him.

[3] **How does Jesus's response differ from what the woman anticipated? What does that tell us about Jesus?**

If we were around Jesus in the middle of the crowd, it would be completely natural for us to want Jesus to give the woman a lecture. She was unclean (bleeding did that to a person under Jewish ritual law), she was a woman approaching him in public, and she took his power without asking.

But that's not at all how Jesus responds. Instead he sees the courageous faith of a woman who'd risked everything she had to be made well, lost it all, and who was now coming to Jesus with confidence. That confidence was built only on what she'd heard about Jesus, but it was enough. In the end Jesus praised the woman for her faith.

Maybe you're in a situation like that woman. Maybe even though you love and follow Jesus, life has been crushing you under its thumb. Maybe you feel like you've screwed up one too many times—that you don't deserve Jesus's attention or help. But the picture we get of Jesus in this passage is a compassionate, loving savior who's waiting to respond to even the slightest bit of faith.

Jesus wants to be with you. As you go through your day, remind yourself of that truth over and over. ∎

3

DAY FIVE

Here we are at the end of the week. We've worked through a chunk of Mark that paints a profound picture of Jesus. He desperately wants to help his followers—all he asks is that they trust that he can and he will.

In the final portion of Mark 5, Jesus resumes his mission of healing the synagogue ruler's daughter. But by the time he's finished speaking with the woman who'd touched him in faith, messengers have already arrived. The girl's dead, they say. Don't bother Jesus.

Before we go any further, stop and think for a moment. [1] **When in your life have you been in a place where you, like the messengers, felt too far gone even for Jesus?**

²**Take a few minutes and do some writing. Or, if you're artistic, some drawing. What words describe that time in your life? What did it look like? Feel like? Taste like?**

³ **If you had to make it into an object, what would that experience be? A chasm? A roller coaster? A hospital bed?**

With that part of your life in mind, let's look at the rest of the story in Mark 5:35–43. Notice Jesus's words to the little girl's father in verse 36. This entire week, people have responded to their circumstances with fear, but Jesus faces it head on.

In the face of fear, Jesus is enough.

In the house (verses 39–40), the mourners laugh at Jesus when he says the girl will be fine. Jesus doesn't lash out or rebuke them, he simply proves them wrong. In the tender words of a loving uncle, he calls the girl awake—out of death and into life.

No one is too far gone for Jesus.

This week we've talked a lot about fear, about trusting in the power Jesus offers us, and about confidence in his care for his followers. Looking back at the moment in your life you wrote or drew about earlier, remember this: Jesus was (or is) there with you.

Take a moment and reflect on the words of the old hymn "What a Friend We Have in Jesus." If you know the melody, consider singing it to yourself. Fear will come in hard times, yes. But alongside that fear stands the one who has the power to raise the dead. Cling to him today. Look to Jesus.

> What a friend we have in Jesus,
> All our sins and griefs to bear!
> What a privilege to carry
> Everything to God in prayer!
> Oh, what peace we often forfeit,
> Oh, what needless pain we bear,
> All because we do not carry
> Everything to God in prayer! ∎

2

3

"

This is not just a bunch of little stories. It's about following the king of the universe who has power over death, over the waves in the sea, over the demons, and says to a little girl, 'Come here, sweetie. Rise from the dead.'

"

SYNAGOGUE IN NAZARETH

06

SESSION 6:

Mark 6:1–29

Through our study of Mark's gospel, we've been getting a clearer picture of who Jesus is and just how much we can trust him. If he's called us onto the road of discipleship, he's shown that he can and will care for us.

So what does it look like when Jesus sends his disciples out to do disciple-making? This week, we'll dig into the main idea that faithful following means doing what Jesus asks regardless of the worldly outcome. There are times when obedience to Christ does not turn out well for us, which is why we should set our sights on something higher than the temporary.

This week, we want to accomplish three things:

- We want to know that following Jesus means sharing in his triumphs and defeats.
- We want to feel free from the burden of believing that we alone are responsible for someone else's salvation.
- And we want to practically strategize how we may share the good news of Jesus.

As we go through this week's study in Mark, keep those objectives in mind.

WATCH: THE GOSPEL OF MARK WITH FRANCIS CHAN, SESSION 6

DAY ONE

★ The Synagogue Church in Nazareth is
the traditional location of the synagogue
Jesus learned at throughout his childhood
and the synagogue he taught from during
his ministry. A Greek Catholic church now
stands above the site.

¹He went away from there and came to his hometown, and his disciples followed him. ²And on the Sabbath he began to teach in the synagogue, and many who heard him were astonished, saying, "Where did this man get these things? What is the wisdom given to him? How are such mighty works done by his hands? ³Is not this the carpenter, the son of Mary and brother of James and Joses and Judas and Simon? And are not his sisters here with us?" And they took offense at him. ⁴And Jesus said to them, "A prophet is not without honor, except in his hometown and among his relatives and in his own household." ⁵And he could do no mighty work there, except that he laid his hands on a few sick people and healed them. ⁶And he marveled because of their unbelief. And he went about among the villages teaching.

MARK 6:1-6

Last session ended on a high note with Jesus resurrecting Jairus's daughter from the dead. Sadly, we can't say the same for the portion of Mark we're studying this week. Instead, we're introduced to various receptions of the message of Jesus, not all of which are positive.

Grab your Bible and read Mark 6:1–6. After a successful initial tour of the countryside, Jesus returns to his hometown for the first time since his ministry began. The people of Nazareth knew Jesus as the son of a master carpenter, but now they meet him as a master teacher in the synagogue.

In the video session, Francis made the point that it's easy to respond to this scene with the benefit of our hindsight. We're shocked that the crowds would reject Jesus. Yet, the same situations occur all around us today. People hear the gospel and dismiss it rather than embrace it.

¹ Think about your own spiritual journey. When you encountered Jesus for the first time, how did you respond?

Maybe you met Jesus as a child through your parents, or someone introduced you to him as an adult. Whatever the situation, there was a time where you had to decide what you were going to do with Jesus's call.

1

² **Now think about the possible objections you might have had (or maybe you did have) to Jesus. What objections to Jesus would you expect from someone today?**

We may not have known Jesus-the-toddler or Jesus-the-teenager-mowing-lawns-in-the-summer. But if we're being honest, all of us have had some kind of issue we've had to overcome with Jesus—even if, as with the disciples, it showed up after we'd decided to follow him.

As we move farther into this week's study of Mark, we're going to discover that part of the road of discipleship includes sharing in Jesus's mission. That means we're going to be taking his gospel to other people. We'll face the same rejection or acceptance that Jesus did.

Take this moment to pray and thank God that he removed the obstacles that might have prevented you from trusting in Jesus. Then ask that he would give you the same compassion for the lost that Jesus showed, despite rejection. ∎

2

"

If you believe in Jesus Christ

right now, that was something

God handed to you. That was

a gift. It was a free gift of his

grace. It's not because you were

some super-spiritual person.

Otherwise it wouldn't be

grace.

"

DAY TWO

1

Yesterday we looked at the reception Jesus got in his hometown. The carpenter-turned-rabbi preached in the synagogue and the town thoroughly rejected him. Like his family in chapter 4, the people of Nazareth thought Jesus had gone a little too far.

Today we're going to look at the next part of Mark 6 where Jesus sends the disciples out to practice what he's taught them. At this point in their discipleship journey, they've seen both the success and failure of the message.

Read Mark 6:7–13.

[1] **As you read, look for details that mirror the way Jesus has already shown his disciples how to spread the message of the coming kingdom. Write down what you notice.**

So far in the Gospel of Mark, the disciples have seen a lot. They saw the beginning of Jesus's ministry drawing huge crowds. They saw Jesus heal all kinds of illnesses and even conquer death. They heard his message to both desperate sinners and hardened religious leaders.

Now it's their turn. Pairing them up, Jesus sends the disciples out on a mission to spread the same message of repentance that John the Baptist did: "Jesus is here. What are you going to do with him?"

Every step of the discipleship journey has prepared them for some part of their own mission. Jesus protecting and providing for the disciples helps them build confidence in not taking any extra supplies. Jesus's power over sickness and the demonic world helps them build confidence in pushing back the kingdom of darkness in his name.

And Jesus's response to those who both accept and reject his message helps build confidence in knowing that the success of their mission doesn't ultimately depend on them.

So, what does this mean for us? In light of Mark 6:7–13, how should we live today? Jesus doesn't wait until the end of Mark to send the disciples out to spread the message of the kingdom of God. We're only in chapter 6 and already the disciples are practicing. Regardless of where your relationship is with Jesus, you have a part to play in his mission in the world.

Take a moment and think of an individual—just one person—that you can talk to this week about Jesus. It doesn't have to be a stranger off the street. You don't have to get them on their knees in repentance. Instead, present them with the picture of Jesus you've seen so far in our study of Mark. Tell that person who Jesus is—what you've seen him do—and leave the rest to them.

[2] **Come back to this page when you've had that conversation and write out a few thoughts on how it went.**

Whether you feel accepted or rejected, know that you're in good company not only with the disciples, but also with Jesus. ∎

2

DAY THREE

Before we get to the final part of our study in Mark 6:1–29, we're going to stop for a moment and look at two words. Mark is an efficient writer. He packs a lot of his message into very little space. As a result, sometimes it's worth looking at the meaning of the Greek words behind his arguments.

We'll look at two of those words. But first, as a refresher, re-read Mark 6:1–13.

In Mark 6:3, we find a word that gives us insight into a crucial aspect of what happens when we share the message of Jesus with others. Mark writes that when the Jewish community in Nazareth heard Jesus teaching, they "took offense." The Greek word is *skandalizo*, from which we get the English term "scandal."

Throughout the New Testament, *skandalizo* often shows up to describe Jewish reactions to Jesus. Sometimes it takes the form of a noun and gets translated "stumbling block" (see Rom 9:32–33; 1 Cor. 1:23; 1 Pet. 2:8). Like Francis pointed out in the video session, the problem with the people of Nazareth was their unbelief in the face of Jesus's teachings.

In a day and age where we're very hesitant to offend anyone, the true gospel is provocative—it always has been. That doesn't mean we should be divisive or impolite when we tell people about Jesus. But we should expect the message itself to come across like a scandal.

One of the biggest reasons (if not the biggest reason) that the message of Jesus is off-putting to some shows up in our second word. In 6:12, Mark says the disciples proclaimed that people should repent.

The word translated "repent" is *metanoeo*, which literally means to change one's mind. In the Old Testament Hebrew, the word is *shub*, which means to physically turn around or turn back. If we take both together, repentance involves both our mind and our behavior. It involves turning our backs on all that is ungodly and turning to face what is pleasing to God—both literally in how we behave but also in how we think.

Mark makes repentance the hallmark requirement for salvation. No one can be saved without acknowledging their sin and clinging to Jesus.

What do we do with this information? The reason the gospel is so provocative is precisely because it demands change. Think about it—people might turn to God when it would mean a change from bad circumstances. But if life's good, why change at all?

Even for us who already accept the message, change is hard. Repentance is still hard. **[1]Take a few minutes and go for a walk. Whether it's around the office or around the block, get moving for a bit. As you walk, every time you get to a turn, take the opportunity to remember what repentance really means. Think about your own relationship with Jesus. What can you repent from? What mindset or behavior can you turn toward instead?**

As you think, remember the confidence we have in Jesus's forgiveness. As we said last week, no one is too far gone. Jesus desperately loves those who come to him. Take that opportunity today. Repent and believe again. ▪

1

DAY FOUR

SESSION 6, DAY FOUR

W e're turning to the last chunk of
Mark 6:1–29 today, and it's a bit of
a sobering story. The section we've been
studying so far has turned the spotlight
on the disciples practicing what Jesus has
taught them.

Today, we're going to look at the first person
who had spread the message of Jesus—John
the Baptist. We'll find out what happened
to him. So, grab your Bible and turn to
Mark 6:14–29.

This section opens by describing Herod's
confusion over the spread of the gospel
of Jesus. Some were saying that John the
Baptist was on his preaching circuit again,
but Herod knew that couldn't be true.
Or could it?

The story flashes back, then, to explain
what's going on.

Read Mark 6:14–20.

[1] **What got John in trouble with Herod in
the first place? Why, despite the trouble,
did Herod keep John around?**

We've seen some poor reactions to those
who shared the message of Jesus, but none
so bad as Herod and his wife. When John
declared their marriage a violation of God's
law, it got him thrown in prison. Herodias
even wanted him executed. Herod kept him
around, though, because of the message John
preached. It intrigued him.

In this short introduction, we get a
microcosm of the reactions to the gospel.
Some reject it and want to squash it. Others
accept it and want to hear more.

1

But the point of this story isn't necessarily to reiterate the various responses to the message about Jesus. Mark's already done that. Instead, he includes this narrative to paint a very hard-to-look-at picture.

Read the rest of the text, Mark 6:21–29.

[2] **What choice does John have in the matter of his life or death? Why does he die?**

John was in prison for the gospel he preached. It had so offended a person of power, however, that it cost him his life. It's a sobering moment in Mark. Sometimes, following Jesus costs us more than a pig farm. Sometimes it costs us our very lives.

The twelve disciples had a chance to practice what they'd learned from Jesus, but for John the Baptist it was the end of the road.

Most of us won't face an angry queen or a militant machete because of our faith in Jesus. But the question we have to answer with each moment of our lives is simply, "Would we die for him?"

We may say we would, but often we set the bar much lower in the way we live. We'll sacrifice a few hours on Sunday morning, or a few minutes each evening for him. But will we sacrifice anything else?

The cost of discipleship—the price of following Jesus—is everything. Up to and including our very lives.

That's a big ask. But it's one that men and women for two thousand years have answered gladly. We can practice giving up everything by starting with something.

Today, consider what you can surrender, put aside, or give away so that you can have the opportunity to show Jesus to someone else. Maybe you sacrifice the comfort of your personal bubble and walk across the street to meet a neighbor. Maybe you sacrifice your leisure time in the evening to call a family member you've stopped talking to. Whatever it is, consider it practice. After all, we're following the one who came to die for us all.

[3] **At the end of the day, come back and write out a few thoughts on how it went. What did you sacrifice? What opportunity did it open up for you?** ∎

2

3

²¹But an opportunity came when Herod on his birthday gave a banquet for his nobles and military commanders and the leading men of Galilee. ²²For when Herodias's daughter came in and danced, she pleased Herod and his guests. And the king said to the girl, "Ask me for whatever you wish, and I will give it to you." ²³And he vowed to her, "Whatever you ask me, I will give you, up to half of my kingdom." ²⁴And she went out and said to her mother, "For what should I ask?" And she said, "The head of John the Baptist." ²⁵And she came in immediately with haste to the king and asked, saying, "I want you to give me at once the head of John the Baptist on a platter." ²⁶And the king was exceedingly sorry, but because of his oaths and his guests he did not want to break his word to her. ²⁷And immediately the king sent an executioner with orders to bring John's head. He went and beheaded him in the prison ²⁸and brought his head on a platter and gave it to the girl, and the girl gave it to her mother. ²⁹When his disciples heard of it, they came and took his body and laid it in a tomb.

MARK 6:21-29

DAY FIVE

We've come to the end of the week, having dealt with some of the more difficult realities of following Jesus. We've seen that his message doesn't always go over well. We've also seen that Jesus invites us to practice the mission before we may feel ready. And we've also seen that following Jesus will cost us.

It's been a heavy week. So, by way of wrap-up, let's do something simple. Take some time and re-read the whole passage we've been studying. As you go through Mark 6:1–29, let yourself simply experience the narrative. We're not asking questions of the text this time. We're not looking for observations or drawing conclusions.

We're just reading it the way Mark wanted us to.

When you finish, spend some time in quiet reflection— just you and God. Start by asking him to soften your heart to his leading and your mind to his Word.

And then listen. Don't pray, don't check your phone, don't get up and grab a cup of coffee. Just sit and listen. Allow God to speak through the words you've read this week.

[1] **After five minutes or so, do some journaling. In light of this week's challenging study, what do you feel Jesus calling you to? An act of repentance? A surrender of your life? A step out in faith?**

Write it down not just as a reminder but also as a landmark—a moment you can look back on where you listened and obeyed. After all, that's how we follow Jesus. ∎

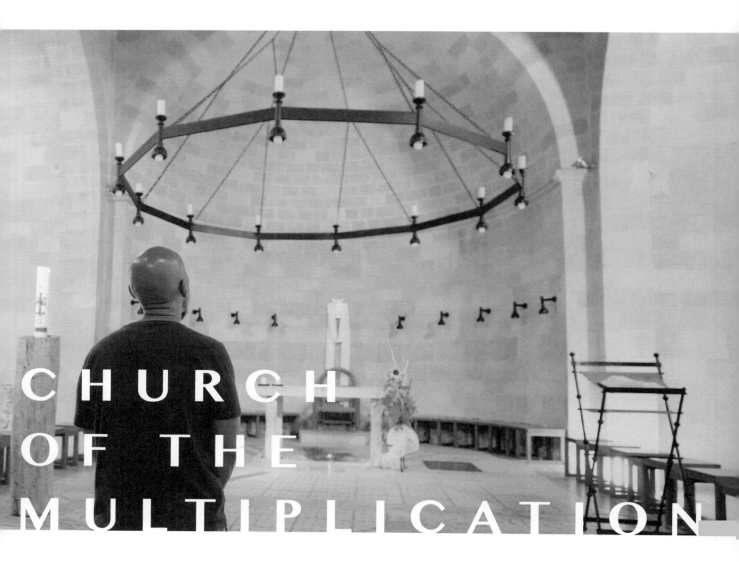

CHURCH
OF THE
MULTIPLICATION

07

SESSION 7:

Mark 6:30–8:30

Welcome back to the Gospel of Mark. This week we're going to be tackling a much larger portion of the book than we have in any of the weeks prior. We'll dig a little deeper into a few important details, but we're also going to aim at what Mark wants us to walk away from this whole section knowing, feeling, and doing differently.

At the heart of this week's study is the unique power Jesus displays in creating something new in the midst of the old and failed. He's more than just a repair man—he's actually making better what sin and darkness broke. The question is whether or not the disciples will understand Jesus's mission.

As we go through this week's study, we have three goals:

- We want to understand Jesus's character and mission.
- We want to feel excited at Jesus's ability to equip us to follow him.
- We want to live in light of our knowledge of who Jesus is and what he's about.

Keep these objectives in mind as we study Mark this week.

WATCH: THE GOSPEL OF MARK WITH FRANCIS CHAN, SESSION 7

DAY ONE

We ended last week on the sobering note of John the Baptist's death. Discipleship isn't always easy, and it doesn't always end in sunshine and rainbows. The kingdom of darkness still wields death against those who would follow Jesus.

This week's section of Mark, however, is going to offer us some hope. We're not following just some charismatic, moral leader. Discipleship means following the God-Man Jesus who holds the very power of creation in his hands. If he has the ability to create and re-create, then we have armor against even death itself.

In the video session, Francis highlighted the important point that Jesus shows that not only can he fix what's broken, but he can also create new things out of nothing.

[1] **Think about everything we've discussed so far in the Gospel of Mark. What difference does it make that Jesus can create newness out of nothing?**

Francis continued his teaching by challenging us to consider the nature of our heart. It can be easy to blame the circumstances of our lives or the bad things we've suffered as the cause of our sin. But the fact of the matter is, we're sinful because we choose to sin—our hearts dictate our actions.

² **In light of that truth, why do you think Jesus has such hard words for the religious leaders? What are they missing?**

³ **What does Jesus want instead?**

We're going to work through this long passage over the next few days. But before we do, spend some time reflecting on what Francis taught and the questions we've asked.

What might Jesus be asking of you today? Will you listen? ▪

2

3

DAY TWO

Today we're going to dive into the text of Mark 6:30–8:30. We're not going to do a lot of digging or reflecting. We want to spend some time getting the story into our heads simply by reading it.

So, carve out a few minutes, find a comfortable spot, and grab something to drink. Put down your phone and turn off the computer if you have to. Then grab your Bible and open it to Mark 6:30. Read straight through to the end of Mark 8:30.

Then do it again.

As you read through the second time, pay attention to how the story makes you feel. What characters stick in your brain? Which ones do you resonate with? What happens that makes you feel happy? What disturbs you?

Paying attention to how the narrative affects us will give us clues to what Mark is trying to say. We're not trying to do deep study at this point. We're just letting God's Word do its work.

As a help, check out the map of the area where Jesus journeys through the passage. He covers a lot of ground in these couple of chapters, and the map should help keep the cities sorted in your mind's eye.

When you wrap up your reading for today, spend some time praying. Ask God to open your eyes to the truths in his Word that he means for your growth in discipleship. ▪

GALILEAN MINISTRY *of* JESUS

★ TYRE

★ CAESAREA PHILIPPI

GAULANITIS

UPPER GALILEE

THELLA ★

★ SELEUCIA

▲ MT MERON

LOWER GALILEE

CAPERNAUM ★   ★ BETHSAIDA

GENNESARET ★

CANA ★   MAGDALA   ★ GERGESA

GALILEE   TIBERIAS ★

Sea of Galilee

★ ABILA

★ NAZARETH

▲ MT TABOR

NAIN ★

▲ MT MOREH   *Jordan River*   DECAPOLIS

SCYTHOPOLIS ★

★ PELLA

SAMARIA

AENON ★

SEBASTE ★

★ GERASA

★ SYCHAR

0 mi   20

0 km   20

DAY THREE

So far this week we've listened to Francis's teaching on Mark 6:30–8:30 and we've read through the text a few times. We've familiarized ourselves with the content and the major themes. Now it's time to really dig into what's happening in these few chapters.

Mark's no slouch when it comes to composition, and our text for this week shows off his literary skills well. In your reading, you may have noticed a repetition of sorts. In fact, Mark 6:30–7:37 mirrors Mark 8:1–30 nearly identically. We see two miraculous feedings, two sea trips, two confrontations with the Pharisees, two object lessons with food, two sets of healings, and two declarations of faith in Jesus.

Mark 6:30 opens with the disciples returning from their jaunt around Galilee and reporting back to Jesus. They then try to get away from the crowds for a breather—they can't even sit down to eat without being interrupted. The crowds follow Jesus out into the wilderness, where he shows compassion to them. It's time for the disciples to learn from the master.

[1] **Look at Mark 6:34–37. How would you characterize Jesus's response to having his recharge time interrupted?**

1

In the feeding of the five thousand, Jesus gives the disciples a chance to come up with a way to serve the crowds. They balk at the idea, so Jesus does it himself. But he meets the need of the gathered thousands by creating something from nothing. He establishes thoroughly that he will provide. Full stop.

As we continue working through the remainder of chapter 6 and all of chapter 7, we see Jesus revisiting not only old stomping grounds but also old topics. Jesus's ability to provide, the nature of true faith, the importance of a soft heart—these and more all come up again. And chapter 8 contains Jesus's offer to the disciples to put into practice what they've learned.

[2] **So, looking at Mark 8, how'd the disciples do? If you were to grade them on their performance, what would they get? Why?**

After reiterating the results of both of his multiplication miracles in Mark 8:20–21, Jesus asks, "Do you not yet understand?" You can almost feel the sadness and confusion coming off the page. All this time with Jesus, and still the disciples are worried about provisions and leaning toward a Pharisaical way of viewing Jesus.

What does this mean for us? In these verses, Mark wants his readers to get a clear picture of just what Jesus was about. Compassion, not judgment. A soft heart, not religious fervor. Hope for both those inside and outside the chosen people, as Jesus takes his message and miracles equally to both the Jews and the pagan Gentiles.

Once again, Mark has a question for us: Is Jesus who we want him to be? Is he the kind of savior we want to follow? Do we get it, or, like the disciples, are we missing something important?

Take a few minutes and do some reflecting. Think about who Jesus is and has been to you. Maybe, like the Gentile woman, you've had times where you came to him longing for his mercy. Maybe, you've had times, like the disciples, where you've missed something important.

[3] **Then write out a short prayer praising Jesus for who he is and asking him to truly see him and his mission. ▪**

2

3

 He didn't come to change our external behavior. He says, 'I'm actually going to change you from the inside out. I can change your heart.' That's the whole story. That's the whole point of what Jesus was doing.

DAY FOUR

Throughout our passage this week, Jesus has been teaching the disciples important lessons about not only what he's doing in the world but also how he wants them to live. Mark gives us a repeated set of stories to double-down on the point—discipleship is all about living the way Jesus lived.

One of the common images in our passage is bread. It gets a lot of play in two different stories about feeding a ton of people as well as being a sore spot with the Pharisees. We're going to look at why.

Mark's playing on an assumption that his readers are familiar with their Old Testament. We're going to take a few minutes and look back at two important passages in the Old Testament that should help understand the nuances of Mark 7–8.

So, grab your Bible and turn first to Exodus 16:9–21. This section picks up after God rescued Israel from slavery in Egypt. The people started complaining pretty quickly, though, because they were out in the middle of the wilderness.

[1] **As you read the passage in Exodus, what sounds familiar to what you've read in Mark?** (Think specifically about the location Jesus takes the disciples to prior to feeding the five thousand.)

1

2 What do you think the people eating the bread Jesus had just multiplied would have thought?

3 If Jesus is re-creating the something-out-of-nothing provision that Israel saw in the wilderness, what does that say about Jesus? What does Mark want us to know about him?

Jesus's provision through miraculous bread should immediately clue us in to two things: First, Jesus is God-in-the-flesh and he will provide for his followers. But second, he's not about simply satisfying our cravings. As the passage in Exodus goes on, God's frustration with Israel grows because, rather than trust him to provide, they ignore his instructions and try to take advantage of his provisions.

In the same way, Mark presents the Pharisees in chapter 7 as also taking advantage of God's generosity, using their own legal traditions to ignore caring for elderly parents.

By the time we get through the second bread miracle, Jesus expects his disciples to have picked up on what he was saying. But, once again in keeping with Exodus, the disciples miss it.

Read Exodus 16:22–30. The Israelites spent an entire week watching God provide miraculously for them, but as soon as it meant taking him at his word, they chose to doubt.

Think about the disciples in the boat after the second miracle in Mark 8:14–21. Like the Israelites, they'd been with Jesus, seen his miracles, tasted the out-of-nothing food. And still they were concerned with lunch instead of Jesus's mission.

This week has us wrestling with the singular question of whether or not we're willing to see Jesus for who he is and follow him in his mission. It's the question of the whole book of Mark, really. In the passage we've been studying, Mark's given us proof after proof that Jesus can and will equip us to follow him.

So, as you sit down to eat your next meal, stop and pray for a moment. In your prayer celebrate the provision that Jesus offers you— not just in the food you're about to eat, but also in the resources you need to be about his mission.

Then, if you have the chance to talk to someone during that meal, tell him or her about the miraculous provision Jesus offers on the journey. ▪

2

3

DAY FIVE

We've come a long way through a huge chunk of Mark. But taken all together, we've seen that the passage wants us to come away with full knowledge of who Jesus is and his ability to execute his mission. But even more, it offers us the hope that Jesus can and will provide for his people in ways that only God has done before.

To follow Jesus is to follow the same God who split the Red Sea and burned the top of Mount Sinai.

[1] **Before we go any further, how's that sitting with you? What's changed in your view of Jesus this week as a result of our study? What are you encouraged by? Challenged by?**

We're going to wrap up this week with a look at the "so what" portion of the text we've been studying. In Mark 8:22–26, we find a rather bizarre moment. A man comes to Jesus to have his blindness healed—fairly routine, right? But it takes Jesus two tries to get him seeing again.

Before we start to wonder if Jesus somehow flubbed the miracle, we have to remember what we've seen throughout the whole passage: two of everything. The doubling-down effect Mark's played with comes to a point here. It takes two intentional actions on Jesus's part for the man to see clearly. Mark's presented Jesus doing the same miracles and teaching twice in our passage. And it all comes to a head now.

Grab your Bible and look at Mark 8:27–30. [2] **After the double effort from Jesus over the last week, what's he hoping his disciples see clearly? Do they?**

1

2

Next week's study is going to put Peter's confession to the test. In fact, Mark 8:22–30 forms the first of two bookends, which make the point that Jesus wants his followers to see clearly—not just who he is, but what his mission ultimately is.

We've asked that question several times this week—do we know Jesus and his mission? Like the blind man, the disciples—with Peter speaking for them—seem to finally get it. But just one conversation later, we'll discover that they still might not be seeing clearly.

[3] As we conclude this week, do some journaling. Based on everything we've discussed this week, how would you describe Jesus to a stranger? If you were in Mark's shoes, what would you write to convince someone of Jesus and his mission?

Next week we'll encounter the final piece of the puzzle to truly know Jesus. But until then, rest in what you've discovered this week. Jesus provides, he shows compassion, and he wants us to follow him. ▪

3

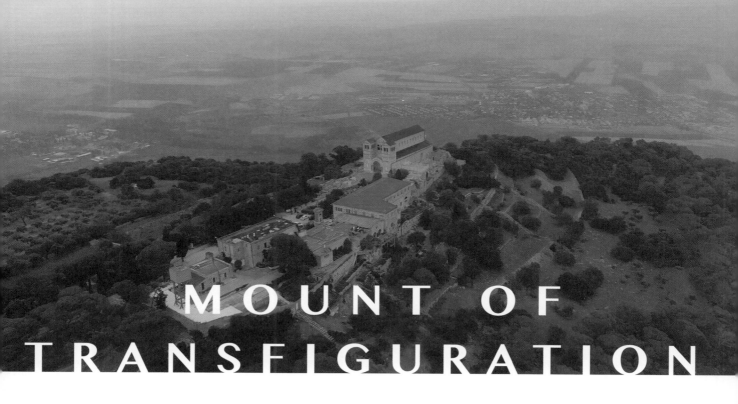

MOUNT OF TRANSFIGURATION

08

SESSION 8:

Mark 8:31–10:52

This week is an important one in our study of Mark. It's the point in the story when everything's made clear. No more confusing parables, no more pressure to rightly interpret Jesus's miracles. For the disciples and for us as readers, Mark's going to lay everything out on the table for us.

And it may not be what we expected.

We're covering a huge portion of Mark again this week, but it's all focused on a single main idea: True disciples of Jesus lay aside everything they possess and all that they are to sacrificially serve like Jesus did.

As we go through this week's study, we hope to accomplish the following:

- We want to recognize Jesus's mission for exactly what it is.
- We want to feel acceptance in light of his call on our lives.
- And we want to listen and follow him in laying down our lives.

Keep these objectives in mind as we study Mark this week.

WATCH: THE GOSPEL OF MARK WITH FRANCIS CHAN, SESSION 8

DAY ONE

What's the most life-changing thing that's ever happened to you? Most of us have a moment in our lives where we knew that something significant had happened. Maybe it was an academic achievement, discovering a talent we didn't know we had, or watching the birth of a child. Certain moments change how we see the world.

This week we're going to find that moment in the book of Mark—the transition that changes everything we're supposed to think about Jesus and his mission. Mark began his book, if you remember, by saying it was the gospel of Jesus the Christ. Despite what we may think as kids, "Christ" isn't Jesus's last name. It's the Greek version of the Hebrew "Messiah." Mark wants his readers to be absolutely convinced that Jesus is the long-promised savior.

As readers of Mark's gospel, we get the payoff moment in Peter's confession. Francis set up the video session by retelling the story. It seems like Peter gets it. If we're following along, we should get it too.

Jesus is the promised savior.

But then things take a weird turn. A few verses later, Jesus goes from accepting Peter's declaration to calling him Satan.

[1] **According to Francis, what was Peter's misunderstanding? How do you think Peter (and, presumably, the other disciples) arrived at that wrong conclusion?**

No matter what Peter said, he still missed what it meant for Jesus to be the Christ. As we go through this week's session, we're going to unpack exactly what the Christ is supposed to do. Mark's going to be explicit with us so there's no longer any doubt.

Before we do, however, we need to read the passage. So, for the rest of today's study, take a few minutes and read Mark 8:31–10:52. Like we did last week, set aside your phone and get away from other distractions. Then just read. Don't ask questions, don't make notes. Just let the story hit you.

[2] **When you've finished reading, answer one question: Based on the passage, what's the real mission of the Christ?** ∎

1

2

DAY TWO

In every good story, there comes a moment when the hero has to die. Think about the last few action movies you've watched. Whether it's Iron Man rocketing a nuclear warhead into outer space or Katniss Everdeen volunteering in her sister's place, a good story has a sacrifice. It's been that way for as long as humans have told stories.

We know it. Mark knows it. But the disciples don't. After their tour of Galilee, Peter seems to get it—Jesus is the Christ. As Francis pointed out in the video session, Peter was expecting a different kind of Christ than Jesus.

So, let's roll up our sleeves and dig into the story. Open your Bible to Mark 8:31–38. Read the passage slowly, and, as you do, look for a few things. Look for the attitude that Francis pointed out in Peter. Look for how Jesus counters that attitude, and what he offers in its place.

[1] **Thinking back to Francis's teaching and looking at what you've read, what about Jesus's statement do you think bothered Peter?**

[2] **What challenge does Jesus lay down before his followers and the disciples? How does Jesus's challenge differ from Peter's implied expectations?**

1

2

Jesus knows full well what Peter and the disciples expect from the Christ—the savior of Israel. After all, the Jews had been waiting for centuries for God's chosen one to come and set them free from political oppression. But throughout the story so far, Jesus has offered the disciples the chance to see him and his mission for what it really is—the overthrow not of Rome but of the kingdom of darkness.

They still don't get it, though. So, Jesus gets super explicit. As with the blind man earlier who took two tries to see clearly, Jesus is giving it another go. This time, he's being painfully clear. His mission is to suffer and die.

What does this mean for us? If the disciples—and we as readers—want to follow Jesus, it means dying. We don't like death. We don't like talking about it. But death-to-self is the destiny of every single person who follows Jesus.

[3] **Take a few minutes and do some journaling. Write out your reaction to Jesus's challenge to follow him and die. What have you already given up in order to follow him? What might you still have to surrender?**

In this week's passage, Mark is going to hammer home Jesus's mission and the challenge it sets before each of us. ∎

3

"

Jesus has just explained
to them, 'This is what it
means to follow me. It
means death on this earth.'

"

DAY THREE

If you've ever ridden a roller coaster (or been in a car accident), you know what whiplash can feel like. The disciples may not have been at Six Flags, but it's not hard to imagine the mental whiplash that comes with the Transfiguration.

Before we get to the text, remember what we discussed yesterday—what Francis highlighted in the video teaching. [1] **What kind of Christ were the disciples expecting?**

Jesus begins chapter 9 with a promise to the disciples that some would see the kingdom of God come in power. Put yourself back in the shoes of the disciples. [2] **What are you anticipating from Jesus after that statement?**

The matter gets more difficult for three of Jesus's closest friends, Peter, James, and John. Grab your Bible and turn to Mark 9:1–13. Read the passage slowly and look for confusion, especially from Peter.

1

2

³ **What aspects of the event on the mountain do you think would lead the three disciples to thinking Jesus had changed his mind? Why?**

This passage re-creates the events of Mark 1 in many ways—Jesus has a special encounter with his Father in a way that confirms his right to be called the Christ—the savior of Israel. But this time, rather than a humble baptism, it's a complete transformation.

That's the future of the kingdom—transformation into something radiant and awe-inspiring. But, like the kid who sees the ice cream come out during dinner, the disciples begin to wonder if they'll get to skip their brussels sprouts. Maybe this whole "dying" business was just a metaphor. Maybe Jesus's transfiguration means it was all just a nice idea.

But then God steps in and states emphatically, "This is my beloved Son. Listen to him." And that's it. No more—the lights wink out and Jesus looks like his dusty self again.

The whole point of the passage isn't to get the disciples—or us—excited about Jesus coming in power to conquer Rome or whatever boogeyman we hope he'll fight for us. It's about God making it absolutely clear that whatever Jesus says, we need to obey.

We're going to do exactly that. So, set this book down and pray something simple, asking Jesus to tell you what he wants from you today. Then listen. Don't talk, don't pray, don't check the time. Just listen.

⁴ **Write down what you hear Jesus challenging you with today, and then obey.** ■

3

4

DAY FOUR

We've talked a lot over the last few weeks about the difficult challenge that the road of discipleship presents. It's not easy. It means surrender, it means loss, and it ultimately means giving up everything to follow Jesus.

Before we go any farther, let's stop for a moment and acknowledge that this is hard. Take a moment to be honest with Jesus and do some journaling. [1] **What's the hardest aspect of discipleship for you? What presents the biggest challenge? The biggest sacrifice to swallow?**

Regardless of what part of Jesus's discipleship journey you're on or what you find difficult, know this: you're not alone.

Take a few minutes and read the vignette in Mark 9:14–29. There's a lot going on in the story. The disciples get fixated on power rather than purpose and fail to cast out a demon. Jesus repeats his demonstration of power-used-for-compassion-not-conquering.

1

But smashed in the middle is a heart-wrenching yet comforting moment. The father of the demon-possessed child knows that faith is the key to rescue. But he needs help. So, he asks for it.

Compare that response to another man's over in Mark 10:17–22. In many ways it's the same request—each man asks something of Jesus. Each time the obstacle is the same: trust Jesus and surrender. But the response is different. The wavering father asked for help in overcoming his unbelief. But the young man left discouraged because he didn't want to surrender his life to Jesus's call.

At the end of Jesus's conversation about rich people entering heaven, Jesus makes a comforting statement, "With man this is impossible, but not with God."

No matter where you're at on this journey of discipleship, you're not on your own. Jesus celebrates in your successes and he's there with a hand of help in your failures. A life of obedience to the savior may seem impossible. Temptations to stray may seem unavoidable. The obstacles to surrender and obedience may seem insurmountable.

But not with God.

Before you end your study today, work on committing Mark 10:27 to memory. As you go through your day, remind yourself that you're not alone. Jesus is with you, and he'll help you in your unbelief.■

[27]*Jesus looked at them and said, "With man this is impossible, but not with God; all things are possible with God."*

MARK 10:27

DAY FIVE

We've come to the end of the week and the end of Mark's powerful argument for the true nature of Jesus's mission. He's here not to overthrow political governments and set up a monarchy. Jesus is here to die.

Our passage for this week ends with Mark 10:32–52. We've said Mark knows his stuff when it comes to literary arrangement, and this passage is no exception. The week began with a two-part healing of a blind man and ends with the healing of a blind man. In between, Jesus states three times that he's come not to conquer but to die. Unlike the first blind man who couldn't see clearly at first, we should now clearly see Jesus's mission for what it is.

But right before we finish, Jesus's disciples have one last request for Jesus. Read Mark 10:35–41.

[1] **What are James and John asking for? What's Jesus's answer?**

1

James and John were there when Jesus was transfigured. They know what he looks like in power and they want in on the deal. Their fellow disciples find out and flip. Jesus, however, turns the conversation on its head.

Jesus establishes a different metric of greatness—not power, but servitude.

PEEK AT THE GREEK *διακονος* | *δουλος*

While describing his expectations for great disciples, Jesus uses two words in Mark 10:43–44. The first appears in verse 43 and is translated "servant." It's the Greek word *diakonos*, where we get our English word "deacon" from. If the disciples want to be great, they must be servants. The word implies the idea of a higher-powered servant in a household—one who might even be an administrator. It may not be the lordly position the disciples were after, but it's not a terrible substitute. But then Jesus chooses a different word to drive his point home in verse 44. There, he says the first in the kingdom must be the *doulos*, or slave, of all. Unlike a servant, a slave in those days had no standing and no rights. He or she was subject entirely to the whims of his or her master. If the disciples wanted to be first, they would have to submit not just to Jesus, but also to each other.

Service and sacrifice. That's what it looks like to follow Jesus. No power. No glory. No fame. Just humble servanthood and self-sacrifice.

Take a minute or two and identify one person you can go out of your way to serve this weekend. It doesn't have to be a grand gesture—in fact, it probably shouldn't be. Instead, focus on how you can surrender your own self-interests to serve someone else.

The promise of glory that Jesus extends to each of his followers comes after we follow him in sacrifice and servanthood. And he's there to help us every step of the way. ■

MOUNT OF OLIVES

09

SESSION 9:

Mark 11:1–13:37

Throughout our study in Mark we've encountered the question over and over: "Do you know who Jesus really is?" This week, we're not going to focus on how the disciples answer that question—although they're starting to get it. Instead we're going to focus on how the Jewish people answer the question.

Remember—throughout his ministry Jesus has attracted huge crowds. But over and over again he tells those whom he heals or performs miracles for to keep their mouths shut. He even wants the disciples to keep quiet. Why? Because he has a different view of power than everyone else.

As before, we have three goals this week:

* We want to understand that Jesus's view of power flips the world's view on its head.
* We want to feel peace in the midst of persecution, knowing Jesus is with us.
* We want to shape our day-to-day lives to always be prepared for Jesus's return.

WATCH: THE GOSPEL OF MARK WITH FRANCIS CHAN, SESSION 9

DAY ONE

Through the whole book of Mark—ever since he introduced Jesus as the "Christ, the Son of God"—we've been waiting for Jesus to truly step into his role as Israel's savior. And so are the Jews of Jesus's day.

Think about it for a second. Here's a miracle-worker who's raised people from the dead and thrown down with the religious leaders of the day, and he's arrived at the capital of Israel, Jerusalem. The crowds have no idea what Jesus is really there to do. Only the disciples heard Jesus's predictions of his death. But the gathered masses are excited, because they think they're finally getting the king they've longed for.

In the video session, Francis painted a picture of the crowd's expectation and set up just how disappointed they would soon be. But Francis also described Jesus's conflict with the religious leaders who ran the show.

For both groups, the one thing at stake is power. The people wanted power given to them to overthrow their rulers, even if that meant the religious leaders. And the religious leaders hated Jesus because he threatened their power.

[1]**Take a few minutes and read our passage for this week: Mark 11:1–13:37. As you read, look for how Mark treats the issue of power: Who has it? Who thinks they have it but really don't? When is power good? When is it bad?**

Write your observations down, along with any thoughts that the text or Francis's teaching may have surfaced for you.

We'll look more in depth at what's going on in this chunk of Mark, but for now, the important thing is to recognize that Jesus is once again subverting expectations. Before wrapping up today, consider the following question: In what areas of your life do you have power? We'll get to how we handle that power later, but for now, just keep it in the back of your mind. ∎

"

The whole town is in a frenzy. This is the time when the king of the universe was supposed to take over the city. But that's not what he does and the people don't quite understand it.

"

DAY TWO

If you've ever watched the movie *Rocky* or seen a boxing match on TV, you're already familiar with the fanfare that comes with contestants entering the building. Each walks down an aisle with the chants of their fans in the air following them to the ring.

Strange as it may sound, Mark sets up a similar picture for his readers in chapter 11. In the opening verses we find Jesus and his disciples preparing to enter Jerusalem—a somewhat convoluted process that involves finding a donkey's colt. Jesus rides into the city amidst the cries of the gathered crowds. But, as Francis pointed out in the video session, the people aren't expecting a suffering savior. They're hoping for a conquering king. Their words in Mark 11:10 make that exceedingly clear.

They want a kingdom again. They want power on their side for once.

The scene concludes in verse 11 with Jesus entering the temple, looking around, and leaving. It's evocative of a cage fighter surveying the arena before the big match—everything in the chapters we'll cover this week takes place in that arena. In fact, a few verses later will have Jesus quite literally throwing down in the temple courtyard, kicking out merchants and money-changers. If you can imagine, the people are getting amped up.

Mark opens chapter 11 this way on purpose. It's almost as if he's giving his readers the chance to get swept up in the excitement of Jesus's ascension to kingship. But if we, like the crowds, get pumped for Jesus-the-conqueror, Mark offers us a chance to check ourselves for a minute.

Grab your Bible and look at Mark 11:12–14. It's a passage that gives everyone headaches. The fig tree stands as a metaphor for Israel and for us. It looked alive but didn't have the fruit that Jesus expected and desired.

12The next day as they were leaving Bethany, Jesus was hungry. 13Seeing in the distance a fig tree in leaf, he went to find out if it had any fruit. When he reached it, he found nothing but leaves, because it was not the season for figs. 14Then he said to the tree, "May no one ever eat fruit from you again." And his disciples heard him say it.

MARK 11:12-14

Mark's inviting us to question ourselves. Take the next few minutes to think and write. Be honest with yourself. [1] **What do you want from Jesus? Does the way you live your life tend to agree or disagree with the answer to that question? Finally, what encourages you about Jesus, who doesn't play power games?**

We serve a savior who isn't concerned about being the toughest kid on the block. He wants to upend our understanding of who wins and who loses, and to do that, he's going to lose in what the world thinks is a very big way. ∎

1

DAY THREE

Today we're going to look at the various contests Jesus fights in the arena of the temple. He's already been welcomed by the people of Jerusalem as a conquering hero, which puts a huge target on his back that every one of the groups of religious leaders is going to try to hit.

So, grab your Bible and turn to Mark chapter 11. We're going to look at four different sections in chapters 11 and 12 to see how Jesus deals with the powerful. As you read each section, identify the power holder who challenges Jesus and note how Jesus dismantles their claims to authority.

[1] **Start in Mark 11:27–33. Who's in power here? What does Jesus do to disarm them?**

[2] **Next, look at Mark 12:13–17. Again, what powerful group challenges Jesus? How does he deal with their challenge?**

[3] **Now read through Mark 12:18–27. Who comes at Jesus? What does he say that nullifies their argument?**

1

2

3

[4] Finally, read Mark 12:28–34. Who steps up to the plate this time? What's the result?

In every instance we looked through, Jesus turns the conversation around on the challengers. With his words, he proves he can take anyone to the mat. The questions each group asked represented the ways they exerted their power over the people—whether through theology or through political manipulations. But Jesus proved over and over again that they were more interested in preserving their power than in actually listening to Jesus.

Until the last scribe. He knew the truth, and his interaction with Jesus in Mark 12:28–34 proves it. But Jesus issues a strong warning a few verses later in 12:38–40 that even the scribes use all their knowledge to exploit the weak.

So, what does this mean for us? What's Mark trying to point out? For those who've begun this journey of discipleship, the reality is we'll face powerful people who want nothing to do with Jesus.

Maybe you have already. If you haven't yet, you certainly will. A boss. A family member. Maybe even a politician. The truth that Mark wants us to walk away with is simple: The powerful persecutors in our lives have no real power over us.

In the next chapter, Jesus is going to promise his disciples that they will face the same rejection and persecution he does. But we have hope! Jesus is with us in the midst of it. He was there before us, and he'll be there with us.

[5] Take a minute and write out a prayer of hope and thanks to Jesus. Thank him for his strength under pressure and the companionship he offers us when we suffer under the powerful. And then rejoice that we have a humble savior who doesn't wield power over the weak. ∎

4

5

²⁸One of the teachers of the law came and heard them debating. Noticing that Jesus had given them a good answer, he asked him, "Of all the commandments, which is the most important?"

²⁹"The most important one," answered Jesus, "is this: 'Hear, O Israel: The Lord our God, the Lord is one. ³⁰Love the Lord your God with all your heart and with all your soul and with all your mind and with all your strength.' ³¹The second is this: 'Love your neighbor as yourself.' There is no commandment greater than these."

³²"Well said, teacher," the man replied. "You are right in saying that God is one and there is no other but him. ³³To love him with all your heart, with all your understanding and with all your strength, and to love your neighbor as yourself is more important than all burnt offerings and sacrifices."

³⁴When Jesus saw that he had answered wisely, he said to him, "You are not far from the kingdom of God." And from then on no one dared ask him any more questions.

MARK 12:28-34

DAY FOUR

We ended yesterday's study by looking ahead to Jesus's promise that those who follow him on this road of discipleship would face the same rejection and suffering that Jesus endured. Today we're going to take a closer look at what that means for how we live our lives today.

Open your Bible to Mark chapter 13. In the first few verses, Jesus curses the stones and buildings of the temple. He won his contest in the temple, and now even that center of power, he says, will collapse. The disciples start wondering when that cataclysmic day will come, but Jesus turns the conversation off judgment and onto the responsibility of the disciples.

Read Mark 13:3–13. Jesus isn't really interested in answering the questions the three disciples asked. Instead, he wants them to focus on faithfully following him. There will come distractions, he promises, that will lead many astray. And more than just distractions, the people who follow Jesus will face beatings, arrests, and death.

Mark wrote his gospel so we would know and not forget who Jesus is. Take this opportunity to write out the story of a moment when you knew Jesus was standing with you in the midst of hardship, persecution, or rejection. Use it as a reminder that he has been and will always be with you.

[1] **Think about your journey with Jesus. What opposition have you faced from others? How have you seen the promise that Jesus makes in Mark 13:11 come true—that the Holy Spirit will be with you and speak for you?**

To follow Jesus is to share in his rejection and sufferings, yes. But he does not leave us on our own. ∎

1

DAY FIVE

This week's passage could very well leave us feeling that the Christian life is fairly bleak. If we're going to follow Jesus, we'll face hardship and suffering. But Mark concludes this section of text with a promise of hope. Not only will Jesus be with us in the midst of persecution, but he will return one day as the conquering king the disciples wanted in the first place.

Grab your Bible and open to Mark 13:24–37. Remember that Peter (whose story, Francis pointed out, Mark is transcribing throughout this book), James, and John were with Jesus when he was transfigured. Now, Jesus promises that one day he will return in that same radiance but with an army of angels at his back.

But in Mark 13:32–33, Jesus challenges the disciples to live every day in light of his return. So, here's the question: Are you ready for Jesus's return? Most of us live in relative comfort, and our routines can lull us into a sense of stability—that everything will be the same until the day we grow old.

The path of discipleship, however, asks more of us. Jesus wants us to shape our lives to look like his—giving of ourselves every day in sacrificial love. That takes intentional thought every minute of the day.

So, here at the end of the week, take a few minutes and think about how you'd respond if Jesus showed up on your doorstep today. [1] **Write out those things you'd be glad for him to discover. Then write out the things you would like to change in light of his imminent return.**

We serve a servant-king. Jesus came not to lord his power over us but to serve us with every scrap of his life. He asks that we follow him and do the same, always prepared to receive him when he returns.

The suffering savior will one day return as the conquering king. ∎

1

GARDEN OF GETHSEMANE

★ While the exact location of Jesus's prayer is unknown, the garden that stands today is certainly the garden Jesus wept in.

10

SESSION 10:

Mark 14:1–15:47

We're nearing the end of our study. This week Mark's going to take us into the darkness-before-the-dawn. It's one thing for Jesus to predict his death. It's quite another for him to face it head-on.

Where Mark has put us, his readers, into the shoes of the disciples for the bulk of his gospel, he's now going to turn the tables. He's going to take us with Jesus right into the hardest part of his mission—a mission he ultimately faces alone.

And there is the foundation of our hope: Jesus accomplished his mission when everyone abandoned him. The promise we have in him comes not from our faithful commitment to him, but his faithful commitment to following his Father's will.

This week we hope to walk away from the Gospel of Mark changed in three ways.

We want to:

- Know beyond a shadow of a doubt that Jesus loves us.
- Feel genuine affection for Jesus.
- Set out to proclaim the wonderful thing that Jesus accomplished for us on the cross.

WATCH: THE GOSPEL OF MARK WITH FRANCIS CHAN, SESSION 10

DAY ONE

Over the course of his time with the disciples, Jesus has shown each of them who he is and what he's about. Despite the disciples missing the point time after time, Jesus still dearly loves them.

In the video teaching, Francis pointed out that Jesus was looking forward to celebrating Passover with his disciples—his friends. [1] **As you listened to Francis tell the story of the Last Supper and the events in Gethsemane, what emotions surfaced in you toward Jesus?**

Jesus knows full well what he's going to face the next day. And he knows full well that the friends that have stuck by him through everything on this journey to Jerusalem are going to abandon him. And yet he still shows them love, promising them that his death is for their sake.

It's tempting to think that, if we were in the disciples' shoes, we'd have stuck by Jesus. They missed the point, but we wouldn't. But the reality is, Jesus knew the truth and chose to love them—and us—anyway.

1

Take a minute and think about the people in your life that you love more than anything. **¹ How would you respond to them if you knew that, in just a few hours, they would betray and abandon you? What would you be feeling?**

² Hold that response and those feelings in your mind for a moment. What does it say about Jesus's love for us that he wants to spend time with us despite what he knows about us?

Do you know that Jesus loves you? We sing it in songs as children, but do you really know that he loves you? No matter what you've done, no matter what you will do.

Jesus. Loves. You.

You may be familiar with the song "Jesus Loves Me." What you may not know is that the song was first a poem, recited by a fictional caretaker to comfort a young boy who was dying. The author of the novel, Anna Warner, hoped that her book would bring comfort to the many families whose sons were facing the imminent American Civil War.

As you read the poem, thank Jesus for his love. ∎

Jesus loves me—this I know,

For the Bible tells me so;

Little ones to him belong—

They are weak, but he is strong.

Jesus loves me—loves me still,

Though I'm very weak and ill;

From his shining throne on high,

Comes to watch me where I lie.

Jesus loves me—he will stay,

Close beside me all the way.

Then his little child will take,

Up to heaven for his dear sake.

DAY TWO

In the middle of the darkness of chapters 14–15 in Mark, a brilliant point of light shines. It's a moment so subtle we could miss it. So, grab your Bible and turn to Mark 14:1–15:47. Read the whole passage and look for the bright spots of hope.

Now look back at Mark 14:3–9. Read the passage slowly: [1] **How would you describe the woman's gift to Jesus? What were the guests at the dinner concerned about regarding the woman? How did Jesus respond?**

1

Mark sets the scene quickly but effectively. He describes Simon as a leper, but he would have had to be healed since no leper would have dined with healthy people. Whether Jesus was the one who healed him or not, we can only speculate, but it's possible that this was Simon's way of thanking Jesus.

Already, then, there's an atmosphere of thankfulness in the dinner, but then a woman enters the scene. To pour perfumed oil over a guest's head at a dinner was a sign of high respect and adoration, which is exactly what she does. But rather than recognize the display of deep love and affection for Jesus, the gathered guests criticize her.

Jesus's response should stop us in our tracks. He calls the woman's action beautiful, because she honored him. Throughout the book, Jesus's expectation for his disciples is that they join him in his mission by serving others. But here at the end, knowing there's little time he has left with his followers, he acknowledges the woman's love and devotion to him.

We've been challenged throughout this study of Mark to follow Jesus on this road of discipleship, but in the middle of all of it we may start to forget who's at the center of the story. Mark started this book focused on Jesus. And here in this little vignette we're reminded that it's Jesus that matters most.

So, in a second, put this book down. Get away by yourself somewhere—maybe go for a walk, sit outside for a few minutes, or even spend time reading one of the Gospels. Whatever you choose to do, intentionally spend the time praising Jesus.

Because sometimes, that's the most important thing. ∎

DAY THREE

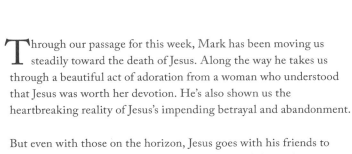

Through our passage for this week, Mark has been moving us steadily toward the death of Jesus. Along the way he takes us through a beautiful act of adoration from a woman who understood that Jesus was worth her devotion. He's also shown us the heartbreaking reality of Jesus's impending betrayal and abandonment.

But even with those on the horizon, Jesus goes with his friends to Gethsemane to spend some time praying. He told them what was about to happen, but they still don't quite believe him—all, that is, except Judas.

In the video teaching, Francis talked about the deep anguish that Jesus finally gives vent to in the garden. Jesus is wrestling with the road ahead of him. And his friends can't stay awake with him for even an hour. In a way, they've already begun to abandon him.

Turn to Mark 14:32–42 and read through the passage slowly. We're not asking any questions of the text this time. Just read it and let the words hit you. The moment that Mark captures here sticks with the writers of later books in the New Testament. The writer of Hebrews in particular has this moment in mind in a couple of passages.

Turn in your Bible to Hebrews 5:1–9. **[1] What do you notice about the way the writer uses Jesus's time in the garden to validate his role as our representative?**

Here's the thing, nothing on this road of discipleship is outside the bounds of Jesus's experience. He knows your pain. That's why he can completely represent us to God. That's why he can stand in our place at the cross. That's why he can weep with us in our own pain.

[2] So, what are you going through right now that you wish you could share with someone? What's making your heart break? Spend some time journaling those thoughts out. Be honest.

Then read them aloud to yourself knowing that Jesus hears you. He's been there. And he's there with you. ■

1

2

DAY FOUR

Today dawns not with brilliant sunlight but with the foreboding clouds of death. We're going to read through the story of Jesus's sentencing and crucifixion. This is where the beginning and the end of the story come together—but not in the way we would have hoped.

Grab your Bible and open it to Mark 15 and read through the first fifteen verses. You can feel the confusion from Pilate in the opening. He knows what the Jews were shouting a few days ago when Jesus entered Jerusalem. And Jesus doesn't deny that he's been given the title King of the Jews. Pilate figures that the only reason Jesus is in custody is due to the envy of the Jewish religious leaders.

So, he offers the people a choice: Jesus—their so-called king—or Barabbas. The Jewish leaders are able to convince the people to call for Barabbas's release. But stop for a moment and look at how Mark describes Barabbas. [1] **Based on Mark's comment in 15:7, what does Barabbas offer the people that Jesus doesn't, or didn't?**

The crowds that followed Jesus, much like the disciples, didn't want a suffering savior—they wanted a conquering Christ. Barabbas the murderer had earned his executioner's sentence in an anti-Rome uprising. He, not Jesus, was the warlike champion the people wanted.

1

But all through the book of Mark, we've seen Jesus validate his claim to be the Christ. The Father himself twice confirmed Jesus as his beloved son. [2] **And yet, read Mark 15:16–32. How did the Jews, the Romans, and the passersby treat the divine king?**

Here at the end of the story, the words that were so sweet in the mouth of Peter—you are the Christ—become a curse in the mouths of all who see Jesus. All, that is, except one.

Look at Mark 15:39. [3] **Who, in the end, understood who Jesus was?**

It wasn't the disciples—they'd run from Jesus's captors. It wasn't the Jewish people—they traded the Son of God for a murderer. It was a pagan, Roman centurion—a man who represented everything the Jews wanted the Christ to destroy. He got it.

Over and over in the video sessions, Francis has been asking us if we really get it. Jesus is the Son of God. He lived and walked in the places we've seen in the videos. He is real. His life is real. His works are real.

[4] **Who is Jesus to you? What does that mean, then, for your life?** ∎

2

3

4

DAY FIVE

We've come to the end of the hero's road, or so it would seem. To conclude this week, we're going to dig into something that often goes overlooked here in Mark's gospel. In his final moments on the cross, Jesus cries out in Aramaic, "Eloi, Eloi, lema sabachthani?"

Other gospel writers record more of what Jesus says and does in his last moments on the cross, but Mark chose only this one phrase. He wants to lean into the true depth of suffering that Jesus endures for our sake—as the righteous payment for the sins of many.

But Mark is also doing something a little more involved here. In the first century, the Jewish Scriptures didn't have chapter and verse numbers. If they wanted to refer to a passage—particularly a psalm—they'd quote the first few words or line.

Mark has in mind not just the despairing words of Jesus as he suffers the full weight of judgment for sin, but also the hints of promised vindication.

Grab your Bible and turn to Psalm 22, the poem from which come Jesus's words. Read through the whole thing, and, as you do, consider how it might summarize the whole of Mark's gospel.

[1] **Then, consider this question: How does the full context of Psalm 22 color the final moments of Jesus's life? What does the poem hint at that should give us hope?**

Jesus was the suffering savior—born to die, rejected by his closest friends and family, and murdered by the people he'd come to serve. Jesus's mission as the Christ was not to conquer, but to show compassion to a world stained by sin. In his faithful obedience to the Father, Jesus purchased salvation for many.

So that, as the writer of Psalm 22 says, "It shall be told of the Lord to the coming generation; they shall come and proclaim his righteousness to a people yet unborn, that he has done it."

As you approach this weekend, determine to tell one person what Jesus did for you on the cross. It doesn't have to be complicated or a come-to-Jesus moment. Simply tell that person what God accomplished through Jesus. ∎

1

THE GARDEN
TOMB

11

We're at the end of the road. We've been trekking through the Gospel of Mark over the last ten weeks, and here in this final week, we're going to bring it all together.

Mark set out to write the account of Jesus in a way that would leave his readers convinced that Jesus was both the Son of God and the long-expected savior. Through a careful retelling of Jesus's teaching, miracles, and life, he has not only shown us the Christ, but also given us the clue to living this thing we call the Christian life.

And here we are. The story's almost been told. This week we're going to look at what Mark expects us to do with it. How should we live in light of the story we've read and digested over the last several weeks?

By way of answer, we want to accomplish three things in this final week of study.

We want to:

- Know that Jesus forgives our greatest failures in order to restore us to discipleship.
- Feel comfort in knowing that no matter our status in the world, we can still follow Jesus.
- Commit to following Jesus on our own road from Galilee to Jerusalem.

SESSION 11:
Mark 16:1–8

WATCH: THE GOSPEL OF MARK WITH FRANCIS CHAN, SESSION 11

In this final session, you'll notice that we're not really discussing Mark 16:9–20. There're a couple of reasons for that we'd like to look at briefly. Mark technically has two endings—the long and the short. Most Bibles will have a note starting in Mark 16:9 pointing out that the last two thirds of the chapter weren't in the oldest manuscripts. The long ending's also missing from over one hundred other manuscripts, and many of the early church fathers write as if they knew only the short ending of Mark. In addition, the tone and style of the original Greek in the long ending don't seem to match the rest of Mark's gospel, implying that it was composed at the very least much later if not by someone else entirely.

So why do we have it in our Bibles? The easy answer is that the large majority of manuscripts do include the long ending, and the early English translations of the New Testament adopted the long ending without question. Despite scholarly argument against the authenticity of the long ending, translational tradition kept it in each new edition of the English Bible. Even now, it's included almost as a nod to that tradition, despite nearly all English translations pointing out that it's probably not original to Mark's gospel.

Should we be worried? Absolutely not. Virtually all scholars agree that the last twelve verses of Mark were added by someone else—most likely as a way to harmonize the Gospel of Mark with the other three gospels. That doesn't take away from the Bible's reliability, but instead shows us the importance of careful reading. Mark has a point to make, and he constructed his book in a very specific way. In order to honor his design, we're going to cover only the short ending of Mark.

DAY ONE

In this last video session, Francis wrapped up the series by asking the important question: If we really believe everything we've read and studied about Jesus, does our life reflect it?

We've called this thing that Mark's taking us through in his gospel the "path of discipleship." It's a journey, really. Mark shows us Jesus walking in a slow but steadfast line from Galilee to Jerusalem. What begins with crowds showering the Christ-figure with praise ends with those same crowds heaping abuse on the head of their crucified king.

Ultimately, however, Mark's not concerned with the crowds. He's concerned with us—his readers. He wants nothing more than for us to be one hundred percent convinced that Jesus is who he said he is. And, if that's true, to follow him on his journey from Galilee to Jerusalem. From servant's life to sacrificial death.

We're not going to go much further today, because we're going to take a moment and consider everything that we've studied. [1]**Take some time to think and then write out your thoughts: how would you answer Francis's question? Do you really believe this Jesus?**

As you think, also consider: [2] **How has our time in the Gospel of Mark changed your view of Jesus? Even if you were a follower from the beginning, who is he to you now?**

In his gospel, Mark had a goal. As his readers, we have the chance to evaluate whether he was successful in achieving that goal. [3] **So, what questions do you still have that you'd like to find answers for?**

Francis concluded his teaching by saying he hopes this trek through the book of Mark has opened your eyes to the beauty of the Bible. The best place to find the answers to questions you might have about Jesus is in the other gospels. Together, they paint the perfect picture of the divine Son who came to rescue us from the kingdom of darkness. ∎

1

2

3

DAY TWO

We don't have much left to read in our discussion of Mark. Chapter 16 is the shortest of all the chapters, particularly since the "long ending" isn't original to Mark. Scholars are in near-agreement that it was written well after Mark completed his gospel as an attempt to soften the abrupt ending.

Since our goal is to let Mark be the one who tells us the story of Jesus, we're not going to spend any time digging into the long ending, but you're welcome to read it. Grab your Bible and open it to the very end of the Gospel of Mark. Read through the chapter but pay particular attention to the first eight verses. This is the last word of Mark's gospel.

[1] **Who visits Jesus's tomb?**

It may seem like an obvious question, but it's one we need to stop and consider. At the end of chapter 15, right after the pagan, Roman centurion confessed that Jesus was the Son of God, we're told that the only followers of Jesus who stayed with him until the end were these women.

It's the first time many of them get a mention in the book of Mark. They're the silent followers. They're not asking questions, loudly proclaiming that they'd face death rather than abandon Jesus, or itching to overthrow the Romans. Instead, Mark points out in 15:41 that they followed him and ministered to him.

1

Already we saw in chapter 14 that a woman showed Jesus unparalleled honor and devotion by pouring perfume on his head before his death. And here at Jesus's tomb, it's the women who followed Jesus to Jerusalem that come to anoint him after his death.

We shouldn't miss this. The people that society would have overlooked as unimportant or valueless were not only the ones to stick with Jesus to the very end, but they were also the first recipients of the best news: Jesus was risen.

We've discussed the centrality of following Jesus on this journey of discipleship. But in a society obsessed with power and platform and importance, it can be easy to judge the success of our Christian life along those same lines.

But the women's visit to the tomb argues differently. What matters is faithfulness, not power or prestige or popularity. This way of discipleship is the same regardless of who you are.

If you've felt lost or forgotten in popular Christianity, take heart—you may be closer to Jesus than you think. Thank him for his faithful love to you. ▪

"

The disciples fled

and some of us look at that

and go, 'Well I never

would've left Jesus.'

But do you understand

what they were going

through?

"

DAY THREE

The biggest question in the Gospel of Mark is whether or not we get the picture of Jesus and his mission. The disciples stand in for us, the readers, in the story, and they constantly fail to answer well. It culminates, as we saw last week, in the disciples completely abandoning Jesus in his most difficult challenge of all.

Have you ever felt like you've dropped the ball? In following Jesus, have you ever wondered if you should just give up—that you're a hypocrite that doesn't act on what he or she believes, and you should just throw in the towel?

Have you ever wondered if Jesus really wants you anymore?

If so, Jesus has some words of forgiveness for you. Mark wraps up his gospel with the glorious promise of resurrection. Jesus had promised way back in chapters 8–10 that, yes, he would die, but death would not have the last word. Yet the cross cast so long a shadow that even the faithful women assumed that Jesus's cry to his Father would be his last breath.

But Mark doesn't leave us wondering if Jesus can be taken at his word. In Mark 16:4–7, the women find Jesus's tomb empty and an awe-inspiring angel waiting for them. He proclaims the fulfillment of Jesus's promise: He. Is. Not. Here!

The angel then instructs the women to tell Jesus's disciples the news. But in verse 7 we find an interesting wording: "Go tell his disciples and Peter."

[1] **Why do you think the angel would go out of his way to name Peter specifically?**

The disciples had abandoned Jesus, but Peter had gone out of his way to deny he knew Jesus three times. It's not hard to put ourselves in his shoes after that kind of failure. But here the angel has a specific message from the risen Jesus for Peter: Jesus still wants him.

Take a moment to do some journaling. [2] **What are you holding in your heart that you believe might be too much for Jesus to forgive? Write that down, and then below it write out in your own words the truth that, if Jesus can forgive Peter, he can forgive you.** ∎

1

2

"

The Bible says that

the Spirit of him

who raised Christ from

the dead

now dwells in

you.

"

DAY FOUR

Over the last few days we've begun pulling together some of the remaining threads in Mark's gospel. Today, we're going to look at the most important one. From the beginning, we said that Jesus was taking his disciples on a journey of discipleship. That trek was both literal and metaphorical. The metaphorical sense was fairly apparent—the disciples went with Jesus everywhere and watched his every move. They learned from him what it meant to be about the business of God's kingdom—serving sacrificially in order to proclaim the supremacy of Jesus.

But that journey was also literal. The other gospels show Jesus making a few different trips from Galilee to Jerusalem and back over the course of his ministry. Mark, however, chooses to portray Jesus's ministry as a single journey—from the place of life and miracles to the location of death and sacrifice.

In the short and rather startling ending to his gospel, Mark records the words of the angel at the tomb. Look at Mark 16:7. Jesus had promised Peter in the same breath he'd predicted that Peter would deny him that, after Jesus had risen, he would go ahead of the disciples back to Galilee. And here in the mouth of the angel, Jesus reaffirms his promise: "I'm going back to Galilee."

Galilee is where it all started. The journey began there. But the implication Mark's making is far heavier than a simple homecoming. He's asking his readers to join the disciples and begin the road themselves.

Jesus had walked from Galilee to Jerusalem, faithful to his Father, and died for the sins of many. Now it's the disciples' turn to walk that road, not just as disciples but also as disciple-makers.

So, here's the question: Are you ready to walk the road from Galilee to Jerusalem? From life to self-sacrificial death, so that others may know Jesus? Are you willing to bring people along with you and show them the way to follow Jesus?

Spend the next few minutes talking to Jesus. Ask him to give you the power and courage to follow in his footsteps. Ask him to open your eyes to other people you can invite onto the road of discipleship with you. ∎

DAY FIVE

So, here we are at the end of the journey. It's been eleven weeks and sixteen chapters. We've come face-to-face with the person of Jesus the Christ. There's one big question remaining.

What are you going to do now?

Mark wraps up his gospel by telling us that the women scattered from the empty tomb and kept their mouths shut because they were afraid. Throughout the story, even Jesus's closest friends responded to his power and mission in fear. So, Mark's asking us what we're going to do. Be silent and afraid? Or be confident in the knowledge that we serve the God-Man Jesus who paid the price for our redemption?

The choice is yours to make, and only you can decide. [1]**Take a few minutes here at the end of this study and write out what you believe your next step is**.

Maybe it's simply getting right with Jesus like Peter needed to. Maybe it's willingly forsaking the distractions keeping you from following Jesus wholeheartedly. Maybe it's engaging with someone else who needs to know the gospel. Maybe it's embracing the truth of Jesus for the first time yourself.

Whatever it is, take a minute and write it down. And then spend time with Jesus in prayer.

We've begun each week by identifying our goals for change. This whole study is pointless if we don't walk away changed by God's Word. The Christ has come. He died. He rose again. So, what are you going to do now? ∎

1

THE GOSPEL OF

MARK

Members of the RightNow team involved in creating this video Bible study
and study guide include:

Brian Mosley: President
Phil Warner: VP, Video Production
Paul Lanum: VP, Publishing & Conferences
Matt Wood: VP, Marketing
Jackie Mosley: Sr. Publisher
Will Irwin: Sr. Producer
Josh Holden: Sr. Producer
Chad Madden: Sr. Producer, Cinematography
Mark Blitch: Producer, Cinematography
Brendon Lankford: Producer
Bradley Van Strien: Field Producer
Courtney Davis: Field Producer
Jason Jean: Field Producer
Clint Loveness: Field Producer
Cameron Rhodes: Field Producer, Cinematography, Colorist
Lee Sherman: Field Producer, After Effects Compositing
Austin James: Field Producer
Lindsey Bynum: Field Producer
Lindsie Herring: Field Producer
Mark Weaver: Field Producer
Jed Ostoich: Associate Publisher, Writer
Collin Huber: Writer
Sophie DeMuth: Copy Editor
Mike Marshall: Creative Director
Jeff Smith: Graphic Designer
Jared Tohlen: Graphic Designer
Mateo Boyd: Graphic Designer

Say Hello

Facebook
@RightNowMedia
Instagram
@RightNowMedia
Twitter
@RightNowMedia
YouTube
RightNowMediaInsider